SMART STARTUP

THE FINE ART OF BEING
THE DUMBEST ONE
IN THE ROOM

SMART
STARTUP

THE FINE ART OF BEING
THE DUMBEST ONE
IN THE ROOM

TIM J. SINCLAIR

Indigo River Publishing

Indigo River Publishing
3 West Garden Street, Ste. 352
Pensacola, FL 32502
www.indigoriverpublishing.com

Editors: Jordan Thames and Regina Cornell
Book design: mycustombookcover.com
Cover design and author photo by Amy Tripple/Twelve Stones Photography
Cover layout: Dissect Designs

Ordering Information:
Quantity sales: Special discounts are available on quantity purchases by corporations, associations, and others. For details, contact the publisher at the address above.

Orders by US trade bookstores and wholesalers: Please contact the publisher at the address above.

Printed in the United States of America

Library of Congress Control Number: 2019941922

ISBN: 978-1-948080-96-5

First Edition

With Indigo River Publishing, you can always expect great books, strong voices, and mean-ingful messages. Most importantly, you'll always find . . . words worth reading.

TABLE OF CONTENTS

INTRODUCTION

*Never try to be the smartest person in the room. And if you are,
I suggest you invite smarter people or find a different room.*

—Michael Dell, Dell CEO

SINCE IT DEBUTED IN THE EARLY '90S, I'VE BEEN A HUGE FAN
OF THE TELEVISION SHOW FRIENDS. It's funny and well written, it has great character development, and the casting is
stellar. If you're unfamiliar, *Friends* is the story of six young
adults living in New York, who spend copious amounts of
time in a coffee shop and each other's apartments, and very
little time at work or stuck in traffic.

Like every good sitcom, each cast member has defining characteristics that make him or her lovable, but also flawed. For
example, Chandler is funny, but insecure. Monica is hospita-

ble, but controlling. Phoebe is good-hearted, but ditzy. And Joey? Well, Joey is well-intentioned but . . . dumb. In nearly every episode, Joey finds himself trying to participate in a conversation or discussion that is far beyond his capacity. As a struggling actor, Joey once tried to change his stage name to Joseph Stalin, unaware of the Soviet dictator with the same name. He called a useless comment a "moo point" instead of *moot*, claiming, "It's like a cow's opinion, it just doesn't matter." And then there was the time Joey swore the Netherlands was the place where Peter Pan and Tinkerbell came from, and the episode when he wrote down all fifty-six states.

I can relate to Joey.

For the last four years, I've been the dumbest guy in every room I've set foot in. I'm not even exaggerating. Law firms, venture capital conference rooms, technology development meetings, even my own office most days. I've been in over my head in every single one of them. Unaware of terminology, unabashedly naïve, and completely oblivious to what should have been obvious.

In these types of situations, human nature (or instinct) says to hide, to cover up, to pretend. We gloss over our inadequacies, spruce up our flaws, and portray ourselves as smarter, better, or more experienced than we really are. It's a tempting—even natural—course of action. And it's one that can have a potentially devastating impact on your company.

It's embarrassing, but early in my startup journey I lived by the "nod and smile" philosophy. When a lawyer or investor or advisor said something I didn't understand, I would grin slightly, nod approvingly, and pray it would somehow distract him or her from the glassy (and terrified) look in my eyes. Quite honestly, as a college dropout who accidentally created a startup after working for seventeen years in radio, I lacked the experience to realize how little I knew.

There was enormous pressure—both real and imagined—to say and do the right things, even if I didn't know why I was saying or doing them. I felt like I *should* know what I was talking about. I felt like my investors, especially, were counting on me to have all the answers. I felt like successful startups were run by founders who had it all together. Thankfully, I couldn't have been more wrong.

A number of years ago, when I was the producer for a morning radio show in Chicago, my boss (who also hosted the show) used to tell me, "Your job is to keep me from sounding stupid." It was his very concise way of saying, "Make sure I'm adequately prepared for every segment, every guest, and every caller. If there's breaking news, I wanna know. Severe weather? I need it first." His instructions were blunt, but they were fair. No one likes looking like an idiot.

So, I suppose now it is my turn to be blunt.

No matter how prepared you are, no matter how much schooling or training you have, no matter how well equipped you believe yourself to be for launching your own startup, you *will* look stupid. Probably a lot. You'll make bad decisions. You'll hire the wrong person. You won't have all the answers. You'll sit in meetings with that same glassy look in your eyes that I had, wondering if you have the smarts or the tools or the intestinal fortitude to turn your dream into a reality. It's the nature of the beast. And, to the best of my knowledge, it's entirely unavoidable.

The good news is that it's okay to feel that way, and I understand more than most. Hell, this entire book is an outcropping of my own inadequacies, insecurities, and idiocy. In case you haven't realized already, in no way am I a business expert or guru. I'm not the CEO of a startup that went public or a filthy-rich entrepreneur who brokered an eight-figure exit. I'm a guy who had an idea and found a way to make it happen . . . despite being woefully unprepared. And, I'll admit, kinda dumb.

However, as I hope you'll soon learn, being unprepared is hardly the worst thing in the world. Being "dumb" is hardly an excuse to not try. In fact, I wouldn't trade it for anything. Why? Because when you're the dumbest guy or girl in the room, it means you're likely surrounded by people filled with wisdom, experience, and smarts. And a team with these characteristics is exactly what you need to start a successful business.

In reality, the worst thing in the world is not being willing to learn. Not being open to allowing smart, successful people to help you along the way. Not being able to humble yourself enough to risk embarrassment, criticism, or failure. And if you can't get past feeling dumb once in a while, the rest of this book is like a cow's opinion. It just doesn't matter.

Moo.

I

INSPIRATION

You Only Have to Be Right Once

Don't worry about failure; you only have to be right once.

—Drew Houston, Dropbox Founder and CEO

As I drove down the interstate, pulling all of my earthly belongings in a small U-Haul trailer, I was more than a little nervous. I was going through a divorce, had just quit my full-time job in radio, and had literally eighty-eight cents in my new company's bank account. For the next six months I was moving two hundred fifty miles away from my two young boys to join an upstart business accelerator program in Cincinnati, and I was borrowing the truck of my former boss to pull the trailer. Even writing this paragraph puts my stomach in knots.

On several occasions along the journey, I considered turning around and going home, returning the truck and asking for my old job back. In hindsight, it's a good thing towing and hauling isn't my strong suit. My fear of jack-knifing Jeff's new ride doing a U-turn was apparently greater than my fear of going bankrupt trying to live out my dream. So I kept going.

For several years, an idea had been rolling around in my head for a recording application that would make my life as a radio host easier. Much to my surprise, that idea had led me to completely turn my life upside down. Truth be told, my brain always had an idea or two, or twelve, rolling around in it. I was constantly dreaming about one thing or another, and I spent many late nights and early mornings sketching, writing, and designing. Over time I began to feel crazy. I felt like I was wasting copious amounts of time, like I was a serial quitter, a failure, or a grown man with an attention-deficit problem. As it turns out, I was none of those things. I was an entrepreneur.

Entrepreneurs are wired differently than most folks. They have a million ideas, most of which never leave their brains, a couple dozen that make it to the computer or a piece of paper, a few of which are pursued, and if they're lucky, one that actually takes hold. Entrepreneurs push the limits, challenge the status quo, and constantly look for a better or different way.

My entrepreneurship journey began in high school when I started a company called Custom Residential Design. I had a fondness for architecture and spatial planning, so I began drawing floor plans and elevations for a local builder who needed blueprints for financing and insurance purposes. Within a few months, I had actual clients asking me to design real houses for them. Can you imagine? People were placing their family's single largest investment in the hands of a seventeen-year-old. Though I think the front porch kind of fell off of one—not my fault—each of those homes is still standing today.

After high school, however, my attempts at business were far less successful. I tried to create an in-store music and advertising service, launch a resource and design firm for startups, develop a national radio promotions organization, start an online T-shirt store, and get at least a dozen other companies off the ground. None of which ever made a dime.

FORE BETTER OR WORSE

I don't play much golf. It's time-consuming, difficult, frustrating, and expensive. But, every once in a while, I'll get out on the course. It's never pretty, but, occasionally, the barrage of golf balls being hit in the water is interrupted by pure magic. A bombed drive. A chip-in from off the green. A miraculous putt. A glimmer of hope that is just enough to keep me coming back for more—or at least from wrapping my 7-iron around a tree.

I've always considered the entrepreneurial journey to be much like golf. For the most part, it is time-consuming, difficult, frustrating, and expensive. Yet the journey is usually dotted by bits of hope as well. A prototype that finally works—sort of. A potential customer willing to trial your product. A new brainstorm that reignites your desire to create. An investor willing to back your company. All of these things are enough to keep you coming back for more.

Every entrepreneur's journey is different, but, somehow, they all seem to be the same: little successes, followed by repeated failures. Then another small success, followed by more failure. The process can seem never-ending, but bona fide entrepreneurs always manage to overcome this tumultuous roller-coaster ride. How? Through a radical difference in mindset. Entrepreneurs focus on and are inspired by their brief successes. Others focus on and are demoralized by the constant failure. It's that simple.

NEEDLE IN A HAYSTACK

Ideas are a dime a dozen. Successful, life-changing, industry-disrupting companies are not. That's the true challenge for every entrepreneur: finding an idea that is, ultimately, more than an idea. An idea that stands out, sells, and eventually scales. Finding that needle, however, almost always involves digging through a whole lot of hay. Which means you need a lot of ideas.

The beauty of the ideation process is it can happen anywhere. On vacation, in the shower, at work, on your commute. You don't need an office, a white board, or even a computer. Some of my best ideas have actually come while mowing the lawn. However, I recently bought a townhouse, so my creative brilliance is going to have to come from elsewhere in the future.

Bill Gates's idea for Microsoft famously began in an Albuquerque, New Mexico, garage. Mark Zuckerberg's idea for Facebook began in a Harvard dorm room. My idea for RINGR began on the back of a napkin at McAlister's Deli in

Champaign, Illinois. Your life-changing idea could literally begin anywhere, including where you sit right now.

The key is to never stop dreaming, never stop ideating, never stop letting your mind wander into the unknown looking for new, unique, and innovative ways to do things. Give yourself permission to think freely, even recklessly, sometimes. Challenge those around you who say things like "because it's always been this way." Train your mind to question the status quo. Relentlessly ask "Why not?" "What if?" and "How come?" Then, when ideas start to come, embrace them. All of them. Test them. Try them. Pitch them. Pursue them. Your needle is in there somewhere.

TWO QUESTIONS

So, among the constant imaginings in the mind of an entrepreneur, how do you know when one idea is *the* idea? The short answer is, you don't. At least not right away. At the outset, there is often very little difference between the ideas that fail and the ones that succeed. However, there are two specific questions you can ask to help decide whether you should invest significant amounts of time and/or money into one idea over another. And certainly before deciding to quit your job and load up the U-Haul for it.

1. *Is this the right idea?*

This may sound like an overly simplistic question, but it isn't. There are a variety of characteristics that can help determine if an idea is "right." Here are a few to consider:

- **Disruptive.** If you haven't already, you'll frequently hear the word "disruptive." Investors, especially, want to know how your product or service is going to break an industry as it currently stands. How will it disrupt business as usual? Will your product change the way people do something? If so, will these people be willing to switch? And, more importantly, *why* would they switch? Is your idea revolutionary enough to move a significant number of people away from the current market leaders? Does your company have a quantifiable advantage over the competition?

- **Novel.** Truly unique, never-before-been-tried ideas are very few and far between, so if yours qualifies . . . that's likely an advantage. It could be that no one has tried it before because it is truly a bad idea. However, for the sake of argument, let's assume you're on to something. With a completely novel or unique product, the trick is convincing a large-enough group of people that they truly need whatever it is you're selling. The world has survived without it thus far; why change now?

- **Scalable.** *Scalable* is just a fancy way of saying that, once proven with a small number of customers, your idea can easily be marketed, sold, and distributed to a larger number of customers. Is there a repeatable process you can use to take your concept from local audiences to national audiences, and from thousands of dollars in revenue to millions of dollars in revenue?

- **Timely.** The right idea has to happen at the right time. Technological challenges, lack of market readiness, negative public perception, legal hurdles, and any number of other issues can keep otherwise terrific ideas from ever seeing the light of day. In addition to knowing *what*, you have to know *when*.

2. *Am I the right person?*

Once you've found an idea that seems to be "right," the next question is, "Should I be the one to tackle it?" Every entrepreneur's natural reaction is to offer an immediate "yes," but it is important to understand not just *if* you are the right person, but *why* you are the right person.

What makes you more qualified than anyone else in the world to tackle the problem you're tackling? To launch the product you're launching? Why should you lead the charge rather than someone else? What do you as a founder bring to the table that is unique and advantageous?

Here are several attributes that can help put you at the top of the list.

- **Knowledge.** A founder who has experience working in the industry that he or she is hoping to target is more likely to have the knowledge needed to develop the right product. He or she will also have a better chance of getting it into the hands of the right people than someone who lacks experience. Outsiders, generally, can't even correctly identify the right problem, much less come up with an effective solution. If you have dealt with an issue first-hand and subsequently come up with a way to better deal with it, you're way ahead of the game.

- **Connections.** Sometimes, even if you haven't worked inside a specific industry, you've worked alongside it, around it, or for long enough to develop key contacts and connections. For example, thanks to speaking at a number of different radio conferences and events, I had relationships with decision-makers at several large media companies, friendships with leading personalities in both radio and podcasting, and the cell numbers for several editors of leading industry publications— all of which would be hugely beneficial in testing and marketing our product. If you have a list of influential friends or colleagues within your target market, it makes all the difference in the world.

- **Charisma.** Some people just have "it." They are comfortable in front of people, instantly relatable, readily approachable, and have an innate ability to convince strategic individuals to jump on the bandwagon and join the team. While a highly charismatic founder might not have ideal industry knowledge or experience, he or she can make up for that deficit with exceptional fundraising, leadership, and team-development skills.

- **Character.** Often confused with charisma, character is less of what a person is on the outside, and more of who they are on the inside. An old book written by Bill Hybels once defined *character* as "who you are when no one's looking." Integrity-filled leaders who do the right things for the right reasons are rare, but scarcity means they are in high demand. Launching a startup because of the difference that you believe your product or service can make for others is far better than launching one because of what you think it can do for you.

IT JUST TAKES ONE

Over the years, I've bought and sold my fair share of homes. I think it's fair to say that every single time I've put a house on the market I've eventually wondered, "Is this thing *ever* going to sell?" After listing my very first home, I remember relaying that concern to my real estate agent. He said with confidence, "It just takes one."

His point? A lot of people are going to walk through your home. You're going to stage and clean and show this place frequently. Some are going to love the carpet. Some are going to wish there were hardwood throughout. Some will think the pool is an asset. Some will think it's an eyesore. But the good news is you don't have to sell your home to everyone. It's okay if one or ten or fifty people don't like it; you've just got to find the one person who does. And once you do, the rest won't matter.

The same is true with ideas: it just takes one great one. Over time you're going to plan and create and develop a bunch of different concepts. Some will gain a little traction, and some won't ever see the light of day. Some will make you a few dollars, and some will cost you a few. But you don't have to hit a home run with every idea. It's okay if one or ten or fifty don't work out. You've just got to find the one that does, and once you do, the rest won't matter.

II

FOUNDATION

Imagine You're Drowning

Risk more than others think is safe. Dream more than others think is practical.

—Howard Schultz, Starbucks CEO

Read the stories of Mark Zuckerberg, Bill Gates, Elon Musk, and countless other entrepreneurs, and you'll quickly realize there is no one right way to start a startup. No perfect formula for success, no step-by-step instructions that every new venture follows. Don't get me wrong, there are some definite "have tos," some "should dos," and some absolute "never dos," but the scope, order, and even necessity of most parts of the process are certainly up for debate.

As an architecture major at the University of Illinois, I learned early on that foundation matters. A lot. In fact, when a structure collapses, it is often a foundational issue beneath the surface that can be blamed. The wrong materials, incorrect measurements, and/or lack of soil preparation have sunk many otherwise beautiful and impressive projects. It is critical that the foundation *match* the structure being built on it. For example, a two-thousand-square-foot ranch doesn't require steel beams and concrete pilings that extend one hundred feet into the ground. Usually, cinderblocks or a concrete slab work quite nicely. However, set a ninety-story skyscraper on a six-inch-thick piece of cement, and disaster is right around the corner—if not already in the overpriced parking garage next door.

The same is true with startups. The foundation needs to be built skillfully, while keeping an eye on the type of business one is trying to build upon it. Doing a poor job can easily sink a promising project, while going overboard wastes precious time and resources, and skimping virtually guarantees serious (and expensive) issues in the not-so-distant future.

As a parent, I've always resonated with comedian Jim Gaffigan's story about what it's like to have a fourth child. "Imagine you're drowning," he says. "Then someone hands you a baby." I have discovered launching a startup isn't much different.

THE ACCIDENTAL STARTUP

Personally, I wasn't planning on starting a company at all. As I often say, I accidentally started my startup. I had an idea that would make my life easier as a radio host, and hopefully benefit a few other people in the industry as well. What I *didn't* have were any relevant skills for creating such a product, nor did I have $146,000—the amount I learned it was going to cost to build a beta version.

It probably won't surprise you to learn that coming up with six figures to help solve a problem I faced at my *very* five-figure-per-year job wasn't very appealing. In addition to not making a ton of sense, as a life-long employee of nonprofit radio stations, it wasn't even remotely possible. And my bank account would have quickly verified that claim. I found myself at a crossroads. Do I attempt to raise some money and turn my dream into a business, or do I forget it all and toss my dream in the trash can?

THE OPTIONS

I have always lived by the motto "I would rather fail at greatness than succeed at mediocrity." This, of course, means throwing dreams away is rarely an option. In this case, it meant venturing into the great unknown to begin fundraising. I would love to tell you that I began a highly successful Kickstarter campaign or secured a government grant to get the ball rolling, but no. I did what any clueless creative does when he needs money—I called the richest person I knew.

For years, Steve and his family went to the church where my dad pastored. I didn't know him well, but I knew he was an incredibly successful businessman. My goal in contacting him wasn't to ask for money, per se, but rather to get some advice. If I'm truly honest with myself, though, somewhere deep down I *was* secretly hoping Steve would fall in love with my idea over the phone, offer money, and drop a check in the mail.

He didn't.

Instead, Steve pointed me to a venture capital firm in town where he personally had invested some of his money. Serra Ventures, he said, wouldn't likely be interested in seriously talking until I had a proof-of-concept product to show them, but it was worth a call to the company's founder, Tim Hoerr, to see if he had any advice on how to get from where I was to where I needed to be. I should probably back up here and say that, while I had *heard* of angel and venture funds, I wasn't at all familiar with how they worked. In fact, I wasn't familiar with any of the traditional means for raising capital. For reference, the following methods are the most common options for early-stage startups:

- **Bootstrapping.** This essentially means paying for everything by yourself. You dip into savings, get a bank loan, refinance the house, etc., in order to come up with the cash required to move forward. It can be an enormous risk, but, with no outside investors, the founder(s) retains 100 percent ownership of the company.

- **Friends and Family.** Many budding entrepreneurs opt to ask close friends and family to invest in their ideas. It's often an easier sell, with more relaxed payment schedules and interest terms. Generally, however, this round of investment is relatively small

($100K or less). Unless, of course, you have very
rich or very stupid friends.

- **Angel/Venture Firms.** For entrepreneurs looking
  to raise larger amounts of money, angel investors
  and venture funds are good options. These are
  groups of accredited investors who typically
  spend weeks or months vetting (investigating) a
  company before getting involved. Their terms can
  be strict and require giving up a percentage of your
  company (and maybe a board seat) in exchange for
  their capital.

Some of these types of firms raise pools of money called
"funds" and then invest the cash in various companies *for* their
investors. The firm does the legwork, the vetting, and ultimately the decision-making. Other firms allow their investors
to participate in the process and even make the call on which
startups get cash and which ones don't. Personally, with no
money of my own and few well-to-do friends or family members, I chose to take Steve's advice and called Serra Ventures. I
left a message for Tim on a Thursday evening and, somehow,
was sitting with him in his office on Friday afternoon.

HOW TO GET A MEETING

Several years after the fact, I asked Tim why he agreed to meet
with a novice entrepreneur with no technical skills and no college degree. Generally, those three qualities, or lack thereof,
don't get you very far, especially when you're asking someone
for a bunch of cash. Tim and one of the other principals at

Serra, Rob Schultz, explained that, for them, those types of decisions come down to three factors.

- **Industry experience.** My background and life's work were within the industry I would ultimately be marketing to. I had lived the problem and then set out to find the solution. Had I simply been a random guy who came up with a cool idea that was searching for a customer, their answer would likely have been no. But a founder with experience in the field he is hoping to disrupt goes a long way in the eyes of an investor.

- **Recommendation.** The phrase "It's not what you know, but who you know" is absolutely true. My friend Steve was a trusted investor with Serra, and his recommendation of me as an individual (not necessarily as an entrepreneur) was key. All of a sudden, with Steve's referral, my phone call wasn't completely unexpected. It set me apart from the hundreds of others of startups who were simply calling or emailing every venture firm they could find.

- **Location.** Serra Ventures is located on the campus of the University of Illinois, and many of the companies they work with are affiliated in some way with the school. Having lived in the area on and off for two decades—and having several loose affiliations with the university—gave Tim and Rob a certain level of ease and familiarity with me that they might not have had with founders from other cities or states.

Ultimately, though, the most impactful statement Tim and Rob made was this:

"We invest in founders just as much as ideas."

Whoa. That's huge. Does your idea matter? Yes. But you matter too, more than you might imagine. Your character, your qualifications, your motives, your ability to share your dream and rally others around you—all of that is critically important. Most every investor will tell you: startups led by high-quality founders with decent ideas are far more likely to be successful than decent founders with high-quality ideas.

THE MEETING ITSELF

Getting a meeting with an investor is one thing; being prepared for that meeting is another. I was asked to bring all sorts of materials with me. On the phone, I played it cool. Executive summary? Sure. SWOT analysis? Okay. Pitch deck? No problem. But it *was* a problem. A big problem. Executive summary?! I didn't even have a name for the company, much less a plan for it. A SWOT analysis?! I had exactly zero idea what that was. Literally none. Same with a pitch deck. No clue (a baseball thing, maybe?).

Lest you face the same problem I did, here's a quick primer on some of the items you might be asked to bring to an investment meeting:

- **Executive Summary.** Usually a one-page document explaining the mission of your company, introducing the founder(s) and team, highlighting your progress to date, and outlining strategic partners and existing clients (if any). It should also outline how your company plans to make money and show investors why they should want to get involved in your company. Oh, and you'll want to include some contact information too.

- **SWOT Analysis.** The acronym stands for Strengths, Weaknesses, Opportunities, and Threats. Investigating and outlining all of these things is an incredibly valuable exercise for founders, and a required exercise for investors. Knowing what you are best at, what you are not, where you can excel, and who can take it all away from you is critical. And showing potential partners that you, as a founder, have thought this through is equally important.

- **Pitch Deck.** Essentially, this is a slideshow or PowerPoint presentation designed specifically for sharing with investors. It should include much of the same information as the executive summary, but also include details on how much capital you want to raise and how you plan to spend the money once you raise it.

As I mentioned, before that first meeting with Serra Ventures, I had none of this. So I opened up my computer and furiously started typing.

The first company name I thought of, I went with. RINGR. Of course, like any good technology company, I spelled it wrong. RINGR. That was pretty much the only thing I knew about tech—drop vowels. If it worked for Tumblr, Flickr, and dozens of others, it could work for me. Plus, it gave me at least a snowball's chance of getting the dot com (which we later did).

My executive summary was literally patterned after something I found in a Google search and included the idea, the timeline, the costs, the competition, and the marketing strategy. Looking back at it now, it was borderline laughable. Thankfully, my naivete and ignorance were met by Tim and Rob with understanding and patience. And, against all odds, with money.

I've since been told that startup formation *never* happens this quickly and haphazardly—and I've certainly seen it for myself since—but I walked out of the meeting with Serra Ventures on Friday afternoon and had an offer for investment from them on Monday.

THE ODDS

So what are the chances of securing venture capital? Slim, at best. After meeting with the heads of numerous firms, it was obvious that, though the amounts fluctuated based on the size of each firm, the percentages all seemed to be approximately the same. Rob laid out the rough numbers for me:

"We see between five hundred and seven hundred fifty investment opportunities per year. I'd say a vast, vast majority of those—probably 80 percent—come through blindly, either through email or our website. And we'll probably invest in a total of ten companies per year."

To save you the trouble of pulling out a calculator, these numbers mean your startup has a 2 percent chance, at most, of getting a check. I immediately turned to Rob and said, "So the math isn't real fantastic?"

His response was perfect: "For us it is."

And that's really the bottom line, isn't it? The math has to make sense for the people who have the money. The job for those of us who need money is to make our case so compelling, our idea so disruptive, our vision so revolutionary that the math can't help but be in our favor.

SQUISHY SCIENCE

The offer from Serra Ventures was a small $75,000, but it came with a commitment to act as a business advisor for the company *and* help RINGR raise additional money from additional sources moving forward. No surprise, but I had *no idea* what "moving forward" was actually going to entail.

Our first order of business was coming up with our valuation. Simply put, valuation is collectively determining a dollar figure that a willing buyer (investor) of the company and a willing seller (founder) of the company can agree on. For most early-stage startups this falls somewhere between $500,000 and $2 million. The process is what I like to call "squishy science." There are plenty of factors than can raise and lower the value of a startup, including the idea itself, the quality of the team, the size of the accessible market, and the existence, or likelihood, of intellectual property. However, the value of each of these things is truly at the discretion of the investor and founder doing the negotiating. There is no one-size-fits-all formula. And a word of warning to founders: setting your company's valuation incredibly high might seem appealing, and it can be, but going too high with an initial investor can potentially scare off future investors.

At the time of our initial valuation meeting (and this is a recurring theme) I didn't truly understand *why* it was important. Don't get me wrong, I enjoyed the conversation. Two weeks prior I was doodling on a napkin, and now those sketches were worth 600 grand. I like that kind of appreciation. But I quickly learned that valuation wasn't actually the true *value* of anything. RINGR's valuation was really just a way to determine how much of the company my new investors were going to own. With a $600K valuation and two $75,000 investments (one from Serra, the other from our technology team), RINGR was—on paper—worth 750 grand. I owned 80 percent. Investors owned 20 percent.

Fair enough.

BUT WAIT, THERE'S MORE

It didn't take long to learn that no one in their right mind was just going to hand hundreds of thousands of dollars to me. Hand it to a *company*? Maybe. But to a random dude with an idea? No chance. So I had to form an official entity. Thankfully, I had a little (more like a lot) of help. Like a deer in headlights, I sat wide-eyed through a series of meetings with Rob from Serra Ventures and our newly acquired attorney, Alan. Each did his best to speak slowly and use small words, and plenty of acronyms.

While I will outline several of the most common options for company formation below, the most critical piece of advice is this: get an attorney. A good one. Preferably one who specializes in working with startups. Situations vary wildly. Exercise caution. Do your homework. Objects in mirror may be closer than they appear—all that good stuff.

With that said, here's the rundown:

- **LLC.** This stands for "limited liability company." Typically, LLCs are the easiest and cheapest to set up, but many investors don't like to, or just won't, invest in LLCs. Profits or losses from the company flow through to investors or owners, which can have significant tax implications, both positive and negative.

- **C-Corp.** For most investors, the C-corp is the preferred vehicle for their portfolio companies. While the formation of a C-corp is more complex and expensive than for an LLC, it provides institutional investors with more tax protections over time. Some early-stage companies actually form as an LLC and then, when they're ready to begin taking on investments, convert to a C-corp. Again, you should consult with your attorney on this.

- **S-Corp.** This is typically reserved for small businesses that intend to stay small (restaurants, hairdressers, etc.), and for those that do not intend to accept outside investment. The income earned from these companies becomes the salaries of the owners. Chances are, if you're reading this book, the S-corp isn't for you.

Other than spending thirty-five dollars and running a newspaper ad to create a DBA (or "doing business as") company once, I had no experience whatsoever with company formation. But, with the help of a few trusted advisors, we were now incorporating in Delaware, registering with the secretary of state in Illinois, getting our tax ID number, setting up bank accounts, and wiring amounts of money that I had personally never seen in a year, much less in a day. It's embarrassing to admit, but at one point I was signing paperwork left and right with no appreciable idea of what it said or what it meant (please, don't ever do this). But in reality, all those signatures meant that—in less than a month—I had accidentally started a startup.

I had pitched my idea to a tech team and venture fund, secured agreements from both, and incorporated a company whose name I made up on a Thursday night because I was forced to. In all honesty, the process couldn't have possibly gone faster or more smoothly. In fact, in the years since, I've talked with many entrepreneurs who say it took them *years* to get that far—if they ever got there at all.

Decades ago, a family friend told me, "In business, it always takes longer than it takes and it always costs more than it costs." Essentially he was saying, no matter how long you think a project is going to take, plan on it taking longer. And no matter how much you think a project is going to cost, plan on it costing more.

I remember thinking about those words often as RINGR warp-speeded its way from inception to incorporation. And I remember smiling a bit that I seemed to be defying those odds. But it didn't take long for me to realize that RINGR was *far* from an exception to the rule. In fact, we were just a few short months away from becoming the poster-child for it.

III

CREATION

THIS ISN'T THE SCIENCE FAIR

Fail often so you can succeed sooner.

—Tom Kelley, IDEO partner

IN HINDSIGHT, KENDELL AND I SHOULD NOT HAVE BEEN AL-
LOWED TO WORK TOGETHER ON OUR JUNIOR HIGH SCIENCE
FAIR PROJECT. But when the teacher said, "Go ahead and
pick your own partners," we immediately chose each other.
Though we were relatively good students, it was not uncom-
mon for the two of us to be reprimanded for talking to one
another in class. And though we were motivated young men,
we were also easily distracted.

After a few minutes of deliberation, we decided our goal
would be to build a working motor. Ambitious, but doable.

Or so we thought. As I recall, the plans called for several dowel rods, a bunch of copper wire, a large battery, and—as with all good science fair projects—a trifold display board. Our problem, however, did not lie in having the necessary materials. Our problem was having enough time to put them together in any sort of way that resembled an actual motor. Primarily because we started the project the night before it was due.

As you might imagine, Kendell and I were up extremely late wrapping wire, making connections, and gluing construction paper and printed diagrams to poster board. But the science fair project wasn't the only thing we struggled with that night. In an effort to ingest as much caffeine as possible, we also attempted to make coffee. Two seventh graders, with random odds and ends from the local Ace Hardware strewn about the kitchen table, were dumping tablespoons of (what we later learned was) espresso into a coffee pot and trying to drink it. Technically, it was coffee. But it was also more of a solid than a liquid. Perhaps *that* should have been our science fair experiment. Hindsight.

The next morning came far too soon. Kendell and I dragged our weary bodies, rudimentary motor, and accompanying display board into class. Miraculously, it didn't look half bad. The major problem, of course, was that the motor didn't work. At all. Didn't rotate an inch.

FAKE IT TIL YOU MAKE IT

Most seventh-grade boys can barely put their clothes on right side out, so our ability to hide our disaster of a project behind flowery language was limited. However, somehow, we pulled it off. Our presentation was filled with what should or could have been, rather than what was. No, the motor didn't work, but, deep down, we knew it *could* work and with more time *would* work. Through shaky knees and sweaty brows, we did our best to explain why. Kendell and I put our best foot forward, spoke confidently, and hoped for the best. To our surprise, that strategy was enough to earn us a passing grade.

Little did I know, my junior high science fair experience would prove to be incredibly helpful some twenty years later. As a thirty-something with a fledgling startup, a dwindling budget, and a product that didn't quite work, I found myself in a nearly identical situation—but with significantly higher stakes.

TIME, MONEY, AND BUZZ

The problem—and the risk—with nearly every business venture is needing both a working product and a paying customer. You need a thing. And you need people who want to pay for the thing. And it can be incredibly difficult to get one without the other. This "chicken or the egg" paradox is not easily solved, and its ruthless nature has single-handedly sunk more than its fair share of great ideas. But for me, the product (or at least the idea of it) has to be remarkable before you can ever hope to build a solid stable of customers.

A former boss of mine used to remind me frequently that every product or service should offer two of the following three things: price, speed, and quality. One of the three always has to be sacrificed for the other two. For example, speed and quality take money to achieve. Additional employees, more efficient equipment, and premium materials are more expensive, driving up costs for the customer. If you want to lower the price of something, then you are forced to also lower its quality and/or slow down the time required for production. For example, a roofing company can be fast and good, but they're probably rather expensive. A graphic design firm can be inexpensive with high quality, but it probably takes forever to get a final product. A restaurant can serve food quickly and cheaply, but the entrees are probably pretty crappy. You get the idea.

When a startup creates a business model and begins to monetize, the "price, speed, quality" conversation is a critical one to have. However, in the actual "starting up" phase of a startup—while you're still creating the product—there is a different, albeit similar, battle for resources. In this case: time, money, and buzz. Successfully navigating the creation of your product without going bankrupt or crazy (or both), involves some combination of these three things. And the less you have of one, the more you need of the others.

It may be unnecessary, but, so we're on the same page, here is a quick definition of terms:

- **Time.** The physical capacity you have to work on your product. If you already have a full-time job, this could simply be a "nights and weekends" thing. If you've jumped in with both feet and have no other responsibilities, it could be more like an eighty-to one-hundred-hour-per-week endeavor.

- **Money.** The amount of financial capital you have to work with. For some this is a few thousand bucks from a personal savings account. For others this is a five-figure small-business loan. And for a lucky few, this is a few million dollars from an institutional investor.

- **Buzz.** The level and quality of exterior interest and/or support for your product or service. This excitement might be from friends or colleagues in your targeted industry, from organic interest created at a trade show, from media coverage, or from anywhere in between.

Time, money, and buzz are each extremely limited, especially in the formative days of a startup. The challenge for founders is to find a balance that allows their dream to be realized before these available resources are exhausted. The good news is that having just one of these things can lead to more of the other two. An influx of cash can buy you time and buzz. Industry interest can buy you time and bring in money. Not having to rush can save you money and decrease the need for buzz.

By way of example, spending a few hours per week working on your idea in your basement doesn't cost much, but it does extend your timeline for launch and perhaps allows your competition to catch up. Hiring a team to work full time on development speeds things up, but can quickly deplete a company's cash reserves. Exciting your customers about the promise of a new product or service is great, but if development takes too long, the buzz surrounding your product can fizzle. And if it costs too much, the company can fizzle too. You can see the dilemma.

It's truly all about balancing the resources you have and leveraging them to make up for the ones you do not. Do it successfully, and you give yourself a shot. Mismanage the process and staying afloat as a company can get difficult in a hurry. As one of my advisors likes to say, "Sometimes success just means finding a way to stay in business for another day."

PITCHING A PROMISE

At RINGR, we were quickly running out of both time and money. Development was taking longer (and costing more) than expected, and while the idea worked conceptually, it wasn't anywhere close to usable. Generating buzz was the only option on the table.

With the small amount of money we had available, I reserved booth space at a large podcasting conference. Our potential customers would be there, and the goal was to pitch a promise rather than a product. To generate buzz about something that *could* be, rather than something that already was. I paid $800 for a pop-up display, printed some basic promotional materials, and faked an audio demo of what we hoped RINGR would sound like when the product was complete.

For three days, one by one by one, I shared my vision with the hundreds of attendees at the event. I chased down speakers and presenters and influencers, trying to grab just thirty seconds of their time to share the vision. My presentation was filled with what could be, rather than what was. With shaky knees and a sweaty, wrinkled brow, I did my best to explain why. No, the product didn't work yet, but I knew it *could* work and with more time *would* work. I put my best foot forward, spoke confidently, and hoped for the best.

Thankfully, the vision resonated. By the end of the weekend, hundreds of potential customers were excited about RINGR, had signed up for our email list, and were anxious to try out the actual product when it was ready.

YOU ARE GOING TO FAIL

"If at first you don't succeed, then skydiving isn't for you."

I have no idea who said it first, but this is one of my favorite quotes. In addition to being true (and funny), it has a loose application in the entrepreneurship space. If you're not okay with failing (sometimes a lot), then starting a company probably isn't for you, and nearly every entrepreneur or expert in the space will tell you the same thing. It's not a matter of if you'll fail, but rather when.

"Innovation almost always is not successful the first time out."

—Clayton Christensen, Harvard Business School professor

". . . making mistakes is okay. At the end of the day, the goal of building something is to build something, not to not make mistakes."

—Mark Zuckerberg, Facebook founder and CEO

"You don't learn to walk by following rules. You learn by doing and falling over."

—Richard Branson, founder of Virgin Group

"Bad shit is coming. It always is in a startup. The odds of getting from launch to liquidity without some kind of disaster happening are one in a thousand. So don't get demoralized."

—Paul Graham, co-founder of Y Combinator

Thomas Edison wasn't demoralized or defeated by failure. In fact, he didn't see lack of success as failure at all. During his quest to create the first lightbulb, Edison is famous for saying, "I have not failed. I've just found ten thousand ways that won't work."

Henry Ford saw his failures in a positive light too. "Failure is simply the opportunity to begin again, this time more intelligently."

Dreams of a seven-figure payday often cloud the reality of the amount of effort it takes to create an innovative, disruptive product worth selling, or buying for that matter. It means long hours and sometimes working more than one job to make ends meet. It means trial and error, executed with tremendous patience. It means beta testing. And it means—like all of the best-known startup successes—learning to deal with an incredible amount of failure.

FAILURE TO LAUNCH

Creatives generally don't enjoy other people being a part of their process. We hole ourselves up in basements or garages, blinds drawn, trying to get everything just perfect before we unveil our masterpiece to the public. The problem is, unless your name is Michelangelo, this type of creative process is rarely an option.

Modern-day development is trial and error, launch and relaunch, surveys and feedback, adjustments and pivots. And almost all of these iterations are done publicly. That's really what beta means: "We're not quite ready yet, things are probably gonna break, and we reserve the right to make drastic changes at any time without notice."

When the first iteration of your product hits the streets, there will likely be harsh criticism. There will probably be technical problems, and there will definitely be more than a handful of "oh shit" moments. That is not failure, that's normal. You'll never feel ready, and your product will never be perfect. But you aren't painting a ceiling or sculpting a statue, you're building a business.

Startup life is a journey, not a destination. The difference between dreamers and entrepreneurs is launching. You have to launch eventually, and sooner is almost always better than later, even though it can be more than a little uncomfortable. Internal testing and development is critical, to be sure, but without dozens or hundreds or even thousands of impartial eyes on your product in its infancy, there is a very real danger of creating something no one really wants, needs, or is able to effectively use.

When is the exact right time to launch? It's hard to say. But it's likely sooner than you think. While there is the possibility of going to market too soon, the vast majority of startups have the opposite problem. As entrepreneur and investor Reid Hoffman puts it, "If you are not embarrassed by the first version of your product, you've launched too late."

IV

ACCELERATION

SMALL PEOPLE WHO ARGUE WITH YOU

Surround yourself with smart people who will argue with you.

—John Wooden, former UCLA basketball coach

WHEN I WAS LITTLE, I WANTED TO BE JUST LIKE MY DAD. I would sit next to him on the piano bench as he played, would pull up my white gym socks, colored stripes touching the tops of my knees, just like him. I would try my best to "help" whenever he mowed the lawn or raked leaves. I wanted so badly to be like my dad, and, in many ways, I still want to be like him.

But back then, what I wanted more than anything was to drink Dad's coffee. It smelled incredibly good, and, based on the amount he consumed each day, I figured it had to be amazing stuff. I don't know if it was because they didn't want me to get addicted, didn't want to stunt my growth, or if he simply didn't want to share his Columbian roast, but Mom and Dad never allowed me to drink coffee . . . with one exception.

My dad, Gary, is a notoriously slow consumer of beverages (he and I once drove from Illinois to New York, and I'm pretty sure he "savored" the can of Sprite he opened when we left Chicago until somewhere just outside of Pittsburgh). But with coffee, once his mug was finally almost empty, he would let me have the last few, lukewarm drops. Honestly, it tasted awful, but because I wanted to be just like my dad, I choked down the bitter leftovers and pretended to enjoy it. And I did this for the majority of my toddler and elementary school years.

At six foot three, I can safely say those few drops of coffee didn't stunt my growth. I can also say that addiction wasn't a risk either—I still hate coffee. To this day, every cup I've ever tried reminds me of those last few drops in Dad's mug: bitter, brown, and awful.

Fast-forward thirty years and perhaps you can imagine my dismay when—during my very first day at the OCEAN business accelerator—our director, Scott Weiss, gave the incoming class of startups the following words of wisdom: "Everyone you need to make your company successful is just a cup of coffee away."

My head fell, my heart sank, and my taste buds cringed.

IT TAKES A VILLAGE
Before forging ahead, I should probably back up slightly.

Launching a startup requires that someone do the launching. He or she is called a founder, and, obviously, your business needs one of them. Presumably, that's you. But many startups have co-founders, usually two or three people, who share both the risk and reward of the company equally. Often these are friends or colleagues who band together to pour "sweat equity" into the company in exchange for a sizable amount of the company's common stock.

Solo founders retain a greater percentage of ownership in the company, but have fewer people on the ground floor doing the dirty work. Co-founders have to split the available stock between them, but have more heads and hands to help get things off the ground. Plus, they have someone to play ping-pong and air hockey with at 3 a.m.

Less than four months into the existence of RINGR— knowing I was a solo founder and had virtually no business background whatsoever—our lead investor suggested I look into a brand-new accelerator program in Cincinnati, Ohio, called OCEAN. This suggestion came on October 30. The application deadline was the very next day. I filmed a quick video in a production room at the radio station where I was still working full time, filled out the extensive online application, and sent them both off with minutes to spare.

Honestly, at the time, I didn't have the capacity to process what I was doing or why I was doing it. I only knew one thing—the guy who had just written me a large check was saying I should check this place out. So I did.

Just as it takes a village to raise a child, it takes a myriad of folks to launch a startup. Whether you're a solo founder or part of a team, there can still be wisdom in joining a group (cohort) of other companies who learn, work, and sometimes even live together. There are two primary options: accelerators and incubators.

A **business accelerator** is a short-term program for early-stage startups designed to teach the basics of business. The program provides an environment to build the company, surround the team with mentors, and ultimately put the founders in front of potential investors, customers, and strategic partners. This, as I said, is the type of program I attended.

An **incubator** is typically a longer endeavor that involves less teaching, and more working, than an accelerator. The companies involved are often a bit older or established, are trying to "find their legs," and are working to develop and/or launch their product and become profitable. While accelerators sometimes invest seed money, incubators typically charge money to attend.

Of course I knew none of this when applying to OCEAN. I only knew that the accelerator experience was supposed to help my company, and that I would need to quit my full-time job and move two hundred fifty miles away from home for six months if RINGR was one of the ten companies accepted into the program. And we were.

SUGAR AND ICE

As it turns out, Scott's advice about the coffee was 100 percent accurate. It's amazing how many skilled marketers, lawyers, accountants, developers, and fellow founders are willing to invest in the lives of budding entrepreneurs and their companies over a simple cup of coffee. An email, a phone call, a connection on LinkedIn, and five dollars at Starbucks is a small price to pay for the truly invaluable information, direction, and support of people who have been there and done that.

Whether it's a one-time meeting, a monthly get-together, or a working relationship that lasts for years, the ability to consistently work alongside successful, experienced people is imperative. Not only will it provide valuable insight and advice in the moment, you'll be surprised at the future connections that will be made and the surprising doors that will be opened because of these types of relationships.

It can be easy to believe that you (and any co-founders you may have) are the end all, be all for your startup. And ultimately that's true—you make the final decisions. However, one of the hallmarks of a great leader is the ability to surround yourself with people who are smarter and/or more experienced than you are. The surefire way to drive your company (your sports franchise, your country, etc.) into the ground is to assume that you—in and of yourself—have all the knowledge necessary to succeed.

I'm still not a fan of coffee. But over time, and for the sake of my company, I learned to tolerate it. Especially cold, with plenty of crushed ice, milk chocolate, and whipped cream.

FILL THE GAPS

Whether or not you decide to join an accelerator or incubator, it is imperative that you bring smart, successful people into your circle of influence—somehow, some way. People who will challenge you, push you, and help you fill the gaps. There are a variety of ways to do this. Some positions are volunteer, some come with equity in the company, and some are paid, but all of them are important.

Mentors. Available in many different shapes and sizes, mentors for early-stage startups are typically experts in a specific area of business (marketing, sales, etc.) who meet one-on-one with the CEO. Often former founders themselves, mentors tend to donate their time for the sole purpose of "paying it forward." Or, perhaps, in exchange for a cup of coffee every once in a while.

Advisors. Not to be confused with a mentor, an advisor is most often a high-profile, highly experienced business leader with deep roots in the target market of your startup. In addition to offering expertise in specific areas of your business, like marketing, sales, or fundraising, advisors can often add a bit of clout to an unknown startup. Telling investors that you have the VP of whatever at Google or the former retail marketing director at Proctor & Gamble helping guide your company can go a long way. Sometimes giving up a small equity position in the company comes with this, but not always.

Board members. Depending on how a company is legally formed, you may or may not be required to have a board. If you are, then there may or may not be restrictions on how many board members are required and which categories of people (founders, investors, etc.) need to be on it. Usually, the idea is to have board members who can help make industry-specific connections for your company, or who have specific areas of expertise that are needed to succeed. Founders and investors on the board will already have an equity stake in the company. Additional members can be offered one, but it isn't required.

Employees. At some point in your growth, your founding team will have more work than they can handle alone. That is when you consider adding paid workers to your team. Without over-dramatizing it, new hires are one of the most important decisions you will ever make. Whether they're interns, contract workers, or full-time employees, the people you bring alongside you are critical. It goes without saying that finding people who are driven, honest, passionate about your brand, and highly skilled are easy to want but difficult to find. Employees usually want to be paid (surprise, surprise); however, you might also consider a partial-equity arrangement if cash is tight.

DUMBEST GUY IN THE ROOM

It was my time at OCEAN that dramatically reinforced just how limited my business knowledge was, and just how much I needed to learn in order to have a chance at being successful. Looking around the cohort of companies, I saw repeat founders with successful exits, former employees of several of the world's largest technology companies, and many with degrees from prestigious universities like Rose-Hulman and

Embry-Riddle. The instructors and leaders brought in to teach us were titans of industry, holding high-level positions at businesses like Google and Proctor & Gamble and EvenFlo.

Then there was me. A college drop-out with no appreciable business experience and—on most days—no clue what I was doing. My guess is that plenty of others there felt the same way as I did, but for me, there was no doubt—I was the dumbest guy in the room.

During my six months in the accelerator, literally every training session we had was packed with completely new information to me. Though not typically a note-taker, I filled several full-size books with powerful takeaways, detailed sketches, and profound quotes from my time there. As a guy who had opted for a life on the radio instead of in the classroom, my lack of experience with spreadsheets and surveys and, quite honestly, books in general was immediately obvious.

Feeling incompetent is difficult for any entrepreneur. Stereotypically, we are type A individuals—driven, confident, accustomed to success, and unfamiliar with inferiority. Personally, my natural bent is to not even attempt something that I don't feel like I'll be the best at. This fear kept me from playing football and joining the choir in high school, it held me back from pursuing basketball and music in college, and it nearly kept me from starting RINGR as an adult.

Though the journey ahead may look scary or appear painful, I can assure you that it's worth it. Be willing to humble yourself, admit what you don't know, and invite others along to help with the things you aren't equipped to do yourself. If success were guaranteed and the path were problem free, everyone would do it. If the startup road were paved with guarantees and void of bumps, U-turns, and valleys, founding a company wouldn't be called a leap of faith, it would be a step of certainty.

Just be sure that when you leap, you invite a few others to jump with you. And don't forget the coffee.

V

PRESENTATION

MAKE THEM FEEL

I've learned that people will forget what you said, people will forget what you did, but people will never forget how you made them feel.

—Maya Angelou

A DAD AND HIS YOUNG SON WENT OUT TO PLAY MINIATURE GOLF ONE SUMMER AFTERNOON. Approaching the small window to pay for their round, the man said, "One adult, one child please."

The teenage employee responded, "How old is your son? Five years and younger play for free."

"He's actually six, but thank you for letting me know," said the dad.

Slightly confused, the worker replied, "You could have saved yourself some money by telling me he was five. I never would have known the difference."

To which the dad flatly said, "No, but my son would have."

I was a teenage boy myself when I first heard that story, sitting in church as the pastor gave his sermon. He was trying to make the point that kids watch every little thing that their parents do, and they learn how to act through these observations. He could have offered the old adage "honesty is the best medicine," rattled off statistics about the effect truth-telling has on family life, or quoted Bible verses about being honest. And if the pastor had, I can assure you, I wouldn't have remembered the lesson twenty-five minutes later, much less twenty-five years later.

To this day, I still regularly think about that story and the powerful lesson contained within it. I desperately want to be a positive role model for my kids, just like my dad was for me. Though imperfect, my dad was a shining example for me on how to grow into a respectful, responsible human being. He was also the pastor who told that story.

MAKE THEM FEEL

Make them feel. It's the motto I've lived by my entire career. Whether hosting a show, writing a blog, or giving a speech, if I can make my audience *feel* something, the message is going to be far better received. As Maya Angelou so famously said—and my dad so memorably demonstrated all those years ago—they'll never forget it.

In the formative months of a startup, presentations are used early and often. Effectively describing the current market landscape and the disruption your product is about to cause is the key to bringing in capital from investors. It remains critical throughout the process, when updating your board, pitching your offerings to potential clients, and even while attempting to convince top talent to join your team. Telling these folks what you're up to and why is one thing; getting them to feel something about it is another. Thankfully, learning to do so is not as difficult as you might think.

WHAT COULD BE

Presentation expert Nancy Duarte gave a groundbreaking TED talk in 2010 in which she outlined the pattern that—intentionally or unintentionally—nearly every transformational speech throughout history has followed. After two years of research, Nancy discovered that these speeches inspired millions upon millions of people to radically transform themselves, their culture, and their world thanks to new concepts or ideas that were delivered in a very specific way.

Step 1: Tell your audience what is.

Step 2: Tell your audience what could be.

Step 3: Go back to Step 1.

From the Gettysburg Address in 1863, to Martin Luther King Jr.'s "I Have a Dream" speech in 1963, to Steve Jobs's iPhone unveiling at Apple in 2007, every groundbreaking speech throughout history has had this exact same framework. It starts with a lot of what is, then a little bit of what could be. A little more of what is, then right back to what could be. Back and forth, up and down. The current reality, then the future utopia. The plight, then the dream. The problem, then the solution. Until, finally, calling the audience to action, asking them to walk away from what is, and challenging them to embrace what could be.

MAKING THE TRANSITION

Effectively convincing an audience to collectively move in a new direction requires them to understand *why* they should move in the first place. What is the problem? How is it impacting people in a negative way? What are the risks associated with keeping the status quo? Tell stories. Give examples. Pull one or two statistics that succinctly and dramatically help prove your point.

Once you've begun to make your audience feel the true weight of the problem, that's when it's time for a jump to what could be—even if it's just for a moment. Then back to what is for a minute or two. Then what could be again. And so on and so forth until an eventual call to action and conclusion.

When crafting a presentation, it can sometimes be difficult to effectively and succinctly make the leap from what is to what could be. However, there is a simple exercise that can help. Try using one of the following phrases.

What if? After outlining the problem that your target customers are facing, asking "what if" is the perfect way to unveil your solution. For example: What if you never had to feel this way ever again? What if, with a little ingenuity, we could eliminate, avoid, or eradicate this issue forever? What if the solution was just a phone call, app, or inexpensive purchase away?

During investor presentations for RINGR, I played audio from a recorded phone call complete with static, drop out, and delay. It was hard to hear and barely understandable, and represented the tens of thousands of calls I had aired on radio stations throughout my career. Then I said, "What if every recorded conversation on the radio, a podcast, or conference call could sound like this instead?" and immediately transitioned to a high-quality, static-free piece of audio recorded on the RINGR platform. The reaction was always profound. It was immediately obvious to everyone in the room that the problem was real and that our solution was necessary.

Imagine a... This is a quick two-word segue into the utopia you are trying to create. It gives your audience permission to dream with you, to get away from what is, and to think for a moment about what could be. Imagine a hassle-free ticket-buying experience . . . Imagine a world in which you never have to wait to see a doctor . . . Imagine a life without the worry of finding a reputable, qualified nanny . . . You get the idea.

Personally, I used to say things like, "Imagine a time when you wouldn't have to turn up the radio when your favorite personality is interviewing an actor or author" or "Imagine a recorded conference call that sounded as if everyone was in the same room at the same time." The goal is to find a problem your audience can relate to, make them feel the weight of that problem, and then present them with an idyllic solution to that problem.

POTPOURRI

While Nancy Duarte's framework for an effective speech is incredibly helpful, there are a variety of other strategies that can be incorporated into your presentation to help make it as effective as possible. As you follow the "what is, what could be" pattern, you should also:

- **Tell a story.** There's no debating that telling a story is the most powerful way to deliver an idea. It's the power behind novels, films, television shows, music . . . Stories are what move people. You may have even noticed a few extra stories in these pages than you might not find in your run-of-the-mill business book. Stories stick. Information doesn't.

  A 2016 study conducted for *Adweek* found that every time a product had a story attached to it, the product sold for more money than the exact same item without a story. Ilya Vedrashko, the senior vice president and director of research at Origin (the firm that did the study), put it this way: "Stories move not only people, but they also move product."

- **Don't just say it, show it.** When unveiling the MacBook Air, Steve Jobs could have stood on stage and described how thin and light Apple's newest creation was. He could have given specs and details and dimensions. He could have even set one of the new laptops on a table next to one of the old ones to contrast the difference in size. Instead, Jobs held an orange manila envelope in the air with one hand and then casually slid the new computer out of it.

If a picture is worth a thousand words, then a well-thought-out demonstration is worth a hundred thousand. Everyone in the audience at Apple that day *saw* how the new technology was so amazing. Few words were necessary. The manila envelope spoke for itself.

- **Know your audience.** Martin Luther King Jr. did this brilliantly. His "I Have a Dream" speech was filled with songs, scripture, and sayings that were not only familiar to the African American community King was trying to engage, but they were deeply ingrained in the culture. It is imperative that your audience can relate to the problem you are trying to solve and the solution you are trying to provide.

It is equally important that your audience realizes you can relate to them. This means the pitch for your startup might not be the same every time. In fact, it almost certainly won't be. The people you are talking to and the part of the country or world in which you're talking to them will change, which means your stories, anecdotes, and even calls to action might need to change as well.

- **Take as much time as necessary, but as little time as possible.** As a former radio personality, I've heard this phrase hundreds of times from talent coaches and consultants. There is a fine line between not speaking long enough to completely get your point across and going so long that the point is forgotten or lost completely. Don't take twenty minutes to say what you can effectively say in ten. Likewise, don't try to cram twenty minutes' worth of material into ten.

  Think of your pitch as a highway billboard. The job of a billboard isn't to sell a product, it's to intrigue potential customers enough to have them make a phone call, visit a website, or go to a physical store to get more information. Your pitch should be similar. You don't have to answer every question, but you have to intrigue your audience enough to get them to ask a few.

THE LAW OF FIRST IMPRESSIONS

They say you can't judge a book by its cover, but the sad reality is that nearly everybody does. Frankly, it's difficult not to. When presenting, it is possible—perhaps likely—that the superficial outweighs the material, or at least distracts from it. The stories, frameworks, and transitions we've talked about are essential, but much of that can be lost with a less-than-stellar first impression.

You don't need to be a supermodel or a professional speaker, but you do need to be conscious of several small—and easily controlled—variables about your "cover." That way, when investors, customers, or potential employees do judge, they will be left with a positive impression.

Stand tall. Posture is more than just good for your back, it is scientifically proven to increase your confidence, energy, and memory. Plus, it just looks better. As we've already talked about, investors invest in founders as much as they invest in ideas. This means a founder who exudes confidence in him- or herself is far more likely to get positive feedback than one who lacks such things.

A study by Dr. Albert Mehrabian, author of the book *Silent Messages*, found that an astounding 55 percent of communication is nonverbal, while just 7 percent is conveyed through actual words. This means your facial expressions, gestures, and posture are critical to effectively delivering your message.

Speak well. This isn't an admonition to use the Queen's English or to never dangle a preposition. This is simply a reminder to know your material and relay it with confidence. Try not to depend on notes or slides, so you can look people in the eye as you talk. Have a well-thought-out beginning, middle, and an end—for God's sake, please have an end. Or as my dad occasionally says, "Land the damn plane."

One of the biggest problems with public speaking is not knowing how, or when, to quit. This leads to rambling, repetition, and a lackluster call to action—if there is one at all. Know how you're going to get out, and then do it. It is far better to leave your audience wanting a little bit more than for them to wish you had stopped talking five minutes ago.

Smell good. It may sound nit-picky—and it kind of is—but you would be surprised how important smell is. It's yet another piece of the nonverbal communication referenced earlier. A person's scent has been definitively linked to attitude, likability, and attractiveness, and none of these things is bad when it comes to pitching your company. There is no one-size-fits-all scent, but there is one rule of thumb that most studies seem to support: subtle smells are far more attractive than strong ones.

One of my first investment presentations ever was in suburban Chicago, just a few short months after RINGR had been formed. We didn't have a product yet, but we did have a pitch . . . and I had been practicing. There were ten or twelve startups in the room that day, along with several dozen angel and institutional investors.

My speech was scheduled about three-quarters of the way through the afternoon, but, shortly before I was to take the stage, the worst possible thing happened: the computer running the presentations crashed. As several tech guys at the venue worked feverishly to fix the problem, the room sat silent. Well, except for my stomach. It was churning so loudly I felt like I could hear its echo. The entirety of my presentation was on those slides, including audio critical to the "what is, what could be" portion of my talk.

As the minutes ticked by and the crowd grew increasingly impatient, I knew what I had to do. I stood up, moved to the front of the line, grabbed the microphone off its stand, and started talking. With no slides, no notes, and no way to demonstrate my product, I stood tall, spoke with confidence, and delivered the message of RINGR as effectively as I knew how. It is difficult to say how effective my little leap of faith was, but afterward I was surrounded by investors and founders who thought my stripped-down pitch was "refreshing," "powerful," and "engaging."

I don't believe anyone mentioned how I smelled that day, but I can't imagine the splash of Acqua di Gio I was wearing hurt anything.

VI

PROTECTION

It's Not 98 Percent Effective

Playing the patent game well can lead to market dominance, higher business valuations, and financial success. Playing this game poorly can leave you, like the inventor Nicolas Tesla at the end of his life, penniless and destitute.

—Vance V. VanDrake III, patent attorney

WHEN SHE WAS IN THE FIFTH GRADE, MY SISTER AMY WAS ASKED TO "INVENT" SOMETHING FOR A HOMEWORK ASSIGNMENT. Her teacher challenged each student to think of something that would be useful but didn't exist yet, and then to build a model and explain the invention to the class. It was the early '90s, and, having spent her entire life around my dad and me, Amy immediately thought of a television that would help you find your remote control when it was lost.

This was a common issue in our home. I think we looked for lost remotes more than we actually watched TV. Somehow "the clicker" (as grandpa used to call it) would always end up buried in the couch cushions, stuck in a magazine, or underneath the coffee table. Once, we even found it in the freezer.

Amy envisioned a button on the television that, when pressed, would make the remote beep and, thus, easier to find. It was brilliant. And apparently at least one electronics manufacturer thought so too. Less than a year later, Magnavox (I think) came out with a remote-finder feature that was nearly identical. I'm not saying they stole the idea from a ten-year-old in central Illinois, but then again, maybe I am.

MORE QUESTIONS THAN ANSWERS

To protect or not to protect? That is the question. Or one of the questions, anyway. There are hundreds. Is your idea patentable? Is it better to operate with a trade secret instead of a patent? What's the difference? Will protected technology or processes make your company more valuable or more attractive to investors? If you choose a patent, can you afford to enforce it? Will someone steal your idea anyway? If a tree falls in the forest and there's nobody there to hear it, does it make a sound? Stuff like that.

Not to burst your bubble, but I am not here to answer these questions for you. The goal of this chapter is not to give you all the ins and outs of patent law and help you make a decision on what to do and when to do it. There are far too many variables, and far too many options, to try to create a one-size-fits-all philosophy. Plus, my only legal training was the persuasive writing class I took during the second semester of my freshman year in college.

The goal here is to let you know that protecting your company from those who might want to steal your idea or copy your invention is something you want to carefully and meticulously think through, understanding that there are plenty of reasons both for and against pursuing such protection. If ever there was a time to admit that you don't know everything, this is it. The subject matter is so specific, the options are so varied, and the potential risk is so significant that you can't afford to not bring in an intellectual property expert. A skilled patent attorney will be worth his weight in gold. Even if he's really, really big.

WHAT CAN YOU PROTECT?

The first thing you'll need to determine is whether or not your invention is even eligible to be patented. As you might imagine, the US Patent and Trademark Office has a stringent list of requirements that new filings must fulfill in order for a patent to be issued. While you'll want to go over these in detail with your attorney, the following is a list of prerequisites your invention must have in order to be considered.

Statutory. Processes, machines, articles of manufacture, and compositions of matter are considered by the patent office to be "statutory," or eligible to be patented. If an invention does not fall within one of these four categories, you're out of luck.

Novel. If your idea has been seen by the public before, or written about in a journal or article, it is not considered to be new or novel anymore and is, therefore, not patentable. There are a few slight exceptions to this rule, but not many.

Useful. Most all inventions can claim to be useful in some way, shape, or form, and this is the easiest hurdle to clear. However, there are some pharmaceutical and chemical compounds (among other things) that are not seen by the patent office as "useful."

Non-obvious. This can be difficult to determine, but the USPTO says—when compared to prior art (a.k.a. previous inventions)—your creation cannot have been an obvious next step "to a person having ordinary skill in the art to which the claimed invention pertains."

If, after consulting with your team and your attorney about these criteria, you feel like your product or technology meets the requirements of the patent office, you can move from asking "Can we file a patent?" to "Should we file a patent?" And there is definitely a difference.

THE RISK

To help answer both the "can we" and "should we" questions, RINGR enlisted the help of Vance VanDrake at Ulmer & Berne in Cincinnati. With an extensive background in helping venture-backed startups navigate the patent process, Vance and his team were the perfect fit for us. Not only were they extremely knowledgeable and experienced, but they had a heart for "young" founders like me who had no clue what they were doing.

Though it wouldn't be surprising for a patent attorney to have a "file a patent application at all costs" philosophy, Vance didn't. Instead, he laid out the options, helped analyze our position, and then made recommendations on a course of action. There were actually times when it felt like he was specifically trying to find reasons *not* to file.

Vance has written his own book exclusively about intellectual property, called *The Patent Game: Patent Basics and Strategies for Non-Lawyers, Innovators, and Business Leaders.* In it, the patent process is compared to a variety of board games, including Risk, and Vance says deciding whether or not to pursue a patent is similar to deciding whether or not to fight for certain regions in the game.

> *As is definitely the case with new ideas, not all of the Risk territories are created equal. Not every region is necessarily worth fighting for or expending resources—such as time, money, or small plastic men—to protect. Not all of your company's ideas are pure gold; maybe hold off on pursuing expensive patent protection in the Republic of Moldova.*

> *While it can be exciting when something new is developed, it's imperative that you have a sense as to how valuable this prospective territory is before committing your resources. Focusing on a worthless territory can deplete resources and make more valuable areas subject to attack.*

He continues the analogy:

> *In Risk, Asia can appear very attractive because the holder of this giant landmass receives a whopping seven bonus soldiers for successfully holding the entire continent. However, as any*

experienced Risk player will tell you, holding Asia early in
the game is nearly impossible. Other competitors are con-
stantly skirmishing on the edges of the continent, making test
encroachments, and picking off weakly defended countries
to weaken the monopoly. If you want Asia, you need a lot of
resources, and you need to be realistic about how to effectively
use those resources.

Watch out for the Asia equivalent in the patent game. Patent
litigation can seem lucrative in light of highly publicized
$1 billion infringement judgements, as can trillion-dollar
markets like the music or travel industries, but can you target
and hold that much territory?

I was never much of a Risk player growing up, but after reading Vance's comparison to the patent game, I kind of want to
be. Just not with him.

REASONS TO SAY NO

Despite the emphasis often placed on the value of owning a
patent, there are plenty of reasons to decide against it. Not
surprisingly, almost all of them eventually boil down to
money. Accurately determining how much you might spend
versus how much intellectual property "real estate" you can
effectively fence off is key to the decision-making process.

Here are a few reasons you might decide to avoid pursuing
intellectual property:

Your invention doesn't appear to meet the requirements. If your idea or invention doesn't meet the previously mentioned guidelines as outlined by the patent office, any money spent on filing the application is wasted. While it's impossible to know what an examiner will ultimately decide, it's important to do your due diligence to ensure you have a better-than-average chance of pushing large pieces of your filing through.

The initial filing expense is too high. Receiving an issued patent in the United States will easily cost thousands of dollars, perhaps tens of thousands, depending on the size of your company and the scope of your application(s). In addition, patenting your invention in the US is potentially just the first step. Gaining protection in other countries around the world requires additional filings, additional work, and, of course, additional costs.

The litigation expenses are unrealistic. Having an issued patent is only the beginning. You must also have the available resources to defend it in court. Quite frankly, most startups don't have the money to do so, though the hope is to reach a point where you do. For what it's worth, litigating a patent infringement case is infinitely more expensive than the initial filing.

There are too many workarounds. Loosely constructed or ambiguous filings are ultimately just incredibly expensive ways of getting a patent, but not any actual protection. If you can't effectively fence off a large-enough, or secure-enough, area to keep other companies from doing exactly the same thing but in a slightly different way, the fence isn't worth the money.

For example, think about an actual fence. The kind you might find at your run-of-the-mill home improvement store. If you're wanting to keep a Chihuahua in your back-yard, but can only afford a split-rail fence, you'll be sorely disappointed in the results. If you're hoping to block the view of your neighbor's dilapidated car collection, but are only able to put up a chain-link fence rather than a wooden privacy fence, you would be foolish to spend the money. The same goes for patent protection. If the fence you can build won't effectively protect what you want it to, you'll be better served to not build a fence at all.

REAL OR PERCEIVED

Just as there are many reasons you might decide *not* to pur-sue protecting your product or technology, there are more than a handful of reasons to opt *for* it as well. And again, it primarily boils down to money. Owning intellectual prop-erty comes with numerous financial advantages, and these advantages fall into two categories: real and perceived.

Real advantages are the reasons most people want a patent in the first place, including the ability to protect your cre-ation should others decide to copy or steal it. Obviously, once you've created a thing, the idea is to keep others from making money off of that thing (at least for twenty years or so). Most patent attorneys are quick to remind entrepre-neurs, however, that you can't ever keep anyone from doing anything. All you can do is protect your right to defend yourself in court after someone else crosses into your pro-tected territory.

Perceived advantages are slightly more difficult to define, but can be equally as attractive. For early-stage companies, the most common reason to file for a patent (besides the actual protection) is to say you have filed for a patent. Potential investors, employees, and customers each place value on issued patents. They find comfort in the idea that their investment of money or time or trust isn't going to be ripped out from under them because someone else started doing the exact same thing that you are.

One of the most common questions I was asked during my investment pitches for RINGR was, "What is going to stop another company from copying your idea?" Without a patent, it would have been extremely difficult to adequately answer that question. Having one (or at least having applied for one) helps immensely, and can often be the difference between someone writing a check and deciding to pass.

Potential acquirers find immense value in intellectual property as well. While your company will ideally have a thriving, growing customer base and strong revenue numbers to attract acquirers, a thorough patent portfolio can increase the ultimate sales price significantly. And, in the absence of overwhelming sales figures, the right IP can spark an acquisition in and of itself.

THREE RULES

It has been said that the three most important rules when purchasing real estate are location, location, and location. While there are plenty of other things to consider, if you miss on location, your future decision-making won't be as well thought out or as successful as you'd like.

It just so happens that there is a similar pattern for the rules of pursuing a patent: get an attorney, get an attorney, and get an attorney. As VanDrake so brilliantly illustrates, intellectual property is very much a "game," and like most games, you'll play far better when you have someone alongside you who has (1) specifically trained for the game and (2) played it before. The patent game is part chance and part strategy. You can't control chance. But you can control strategy. And if you plan to win, it's critical that you do.

VII

MONETIZATION

A Very Necessary Evil

Business is the art of extracting money from another man's pocket without resorting to violence.

—*Max Amsterdam*

THE DAY WE LAUNCHED OUR VERY FIRST BETA PRODUCT AT RINGR IS A DAY I WILL NEVER FORGET. We had quit full-time jobs, raised more than $100,000, and had worked so hard for so long that clicking a button to post our app on the App Store was cause for celebration. I even took a picture of my computer screen as I did it. The moment was truly a dream realized.

My celebration, however, was incredibly short-lived. Sixty seconds, tops. That's how long it took me to realize that, with a product officially in the marketplace (albeit for free, at that point), our team was suddenly obligated to support it. We still had to continue innovating, of course, but now there were actual users who, for some crazy reason, actually wanted the product to work properly. And when it didn't, they wanted to interact with someone on our team who could quickly fix the problem.

For the better part of eight months our days had been devoted entirely to creating, planning, and dreaming. We spent our time imagining and ideating, designing and deliberating, testing and tweaking. Literally every second was spent on vision, rather than sustainability. On theory, rather than reality. Until I clicked that button.

It took some getting used to, but our team eventually got the hang of devoting resources to both sides of what had become a two-headed monster: development and support. However, as you might imagine, few businesses get very far by simply creating and supporting something they are giving away for free. So, shortly after wrapping our brains around doing two things at once—and in the interest of keeping our business afloat—we were forced to add a third thing: sales.

FIRST THINGS FIRST

In an age when people want everything for nothing, figuring out how to get the maximum amount of money from the maximum number of people the maximum number of times is difficult, at best. For most visionaries (including me), creating and developing a new, innovative product is the fun part. Figuring out the business model . . . not so much. However, it doesn't take an MBA to understand that founders who don't spend significant amounts of time monetizing their products won't be founders for very long. They'll be nine-to-fivers. Again.

At the beginning, the most important thing is to come up with a plan. It might change over time—in fact, it almost assuredly will—but you have to start somewhere. The most basic of questions that need to be answered is this: How are we going to get money in exchange for what we've created? There are a ton of options, but here are four good starting points for most new companies:

1. **Purchase.** This is what the majority of business has been founded on for centuries. You make a product. People buy it. It is the simplest of models and involves a one-time, fixed cost for the customer. Whether it's food or cars, clothing or electronics, customers are presented with a price, and—once they pay that price—the item is theirs to keep and use forever.

2. **Subscription.** Customers pay a monthly or yearly fee in order to gain access to a certain product or service. What used to be reserved for cable television, magazines, and gym memberships has now infiltrated nearly everything. Technology companies now frequently use what is known as the SaaS model (software/security/storage as a service), charging monthly fees for their offerings; however, these days you can pay monthly

for access to everything from audio books to dating sites and clothing delivery to car washes.

3. **Advertisement.** Some businesses choose to give away their products for free and derive their income solely from third-party advertisers. Radio stations have done this for nearly a century, but the ad model has infiltrated many other types of business, especially in the tech world. Facebook, Twitter, and Google are prime examples, but there is no shortage of game and productivity apps that utilize advertisers or sponsors to keep their operations going as well.

4. **Combination.** Quite often, two or more of these methods are used together in order to generate revenue and increase the bottom line. Your favorite game app likely uses a combination of purchase and advertisement, giving you the choice to buy it outright *or* play for free, but with pop-up ads thrown in. Television is another example, implementing a combination of subscription and advertising. You pay your monthly cable or satellite bill, but also sit through ads (commercials) while you watch.

When developing your product, you test and tweak, survey and study, in order to create the best-possible option for your customers. Often, you have to go through a similar process with your business model. While it can be dangerous to change either one too often, it can be fatal to not change them at all. It's a high-wire balancing act, with the same disastrous consequences for failure.

X MARKS THE SPOT

Once you've determined *what* you're going to do, the next step is figuring out how much to charge for it.

Since the plan was to base RINGR on a subscription model, our challenge was coming up with a price that people would be willing, and able, to pay each month. So, we decided to ask them. We surveyed close to one hundred potential customers, choosing a variety of questions not only about how necessary they felt a product like ours might be and what they would be willing to pay for it, but also about other pieces of software they currently used and what they were currently paying for those. The results were mixed and at times felt somewhat inconclusive, but they gave us a general idea of where to begin.

As an aside, there is an inherent danger in surveys. The main issue lies in whether or not people tell you the truth. For example, it's easy to click a checkbox that says you'll pay fifty dollars for something. It's infinitely more difficult to put in your credit card details and actually spend the money. On the flip side, it's only natural to say you don't want to pay very much for a product or service, yet be willing to pay considerably more when you find you absolutely need it.

However you decide to determine your pricing, be aware that the results of your methodology have the power to change your model. Or at least they should. It is entirely within the realm of possibility that millions of people want your product, but you might find through surveys or trial and error that relatively few of them are willing to pay anything for it (e.g., Facebook). While the advertising model might make you billions, trying to sell memberships might make you broke.

Whatever method you land on, the economics of the process are the same. As price increases, the number of customers (or advertisers) willing to pay for it decreases, and vice versa. Let's say you have 100,000 customers who are willing to pay $20 per month for your product. That's a $2 million monthly revenue. However, by lowering your price to $15 per month, you find that you add an extra 50,000 customers. That's $2.25 million dollars monthly. So you should lower your price, right? Not necessarily. It's entirely possible that a $30-per-month fee only costs you 20,000 of your 100,000 users. Do the math, and you realize you could be making $2.4 million with *fewer* customers and a higher price tag.

Imagine a graph with a line ascending from left to right. That's the price. There's another line that starts high and descends from left to right. Those are customers. Essentially, it looks like an X. The goal is to find the point where those two lines meet. That's where you get the highest price from the most customers and, ultimately, make the most money.

THE RISK
In 2011, Netflix CEO Reed Hastings made a highly criticized decision. It might not seem super controversial

now—since we know the end of the story—but back then it seemed risky at best, suicidal at worst. Literally overnight Netflix raised prices by more than 50 percent for many of the company's twenty million subscribers.

At an industry conference in New York City, Hastings said the Netflix mission for 2011 was "Let's not die with DVDs," and it turned out to be a brilliant strategy. (In hindsight, Blockbuster could have benefited from it as well.) With those words in mind, Netflix began offering a streaming-only option in addition to their DVD-by-mail business. Previously, you could get DVDs mailed to your home or DVDs *and* streaming, but not streaming by itself.

The Netflix streaming package started at a very reasonable $7.99 per month; however, the cost for both DVDs and streaming jumped from $9.99 to $15.98. Hastings and his team were going all-in on the Internet. They were betting big that, in a matter of a few years, DVDs would be a thing of the past, and nearly everyone would be consuming video content without the help of a physical disc and DVD player. Their new pricing structure not only allowed Netflix to bring in more revenue in the short term, but it actually encouraged customers to begin adopting the less expensive, more efficient business model.

The beauty is that, even if Hastings's bet hadn't paid off, Netflix obviously knew they could afford to lose millions of subscribers and still break even. My unofficial math shows Netflix could have lost more than seven million of its twenty million monthly subscribers and still brought in more revenue than they had been with their old pricing. Was it still risky? Absolutely. But by working to find the highest price that the highest number of people would pay, as well as betting on a future that most people couldn't see yet, Netflix was able to mitigate their risk then and, ultimately, make a fortune now.

What is the right plan for your business? I have no idea. But I can promise you this: the ultimate solution will be a combination of head and heart, of fact and feeling, of potential reward and undeniable risk. But it's good to have options. Some companies don't, and it is far worse to have difficult decisions to make than no decisions at all. Just ask Blockbuster.

VIII

DISTRIBUTION

THE FASTEST WAY TO GO BROKE

*Every sale has five basic obstacles: no need, no money, no hurry,
no desire, no trust.*

—*Zig Ziglar*

HAVING SPENT MUCH OF MY CAREER WORKING IN RADIO,
I HELPED PUT ON DOZENS—MAYBE EVEN HUNDREDS—OF
CONCERTS. It seemed easy. Likely because other people did
most of the hard work. I wrote and produced ads for the
shows, helped set up seating and sound equipment on occa-
sion, and often emceed the evening from the stage. Nothing
more. However, despite my less than adequate skills and
experience, I decided one day to try promoting a concert
completely on my own.

With numerous contacts in Nashville, I found a tour that was scheduled to come through my town. Without naming names, it was a Christmas show by a group known predominantly for their Christmas songs. There was even an annual holiday television special produced exclusively around one of their hits. To top it all off, the historic theater downtown was available on the date in question, and there were no other shows in the area to compete. It seemed like nothing could go wrong.

Do you remember in the legendary baseball movie *Field of Dreams* where Kevin Costner hears, "If you build it, they will come"? Well, this scenario felt like that to me. I had the vision, the dream, and the necessary pieces for success. All I had to do was spend the money required to put them all together. I just had to build it.

Except that when I "built it," I offered full price for the tour (which was stupid), and I didn't get any sponsors (also stupid). I made assumptions about the media outlets that would help promote the show (I know, I know), and I tried to do (and pay for) pretty much everything myself. Also, I didn't tell my then wife about it. It was a recipe for disaster, and, unfortunately, the recipe worked to perfection.

Food, crew, and production costs were higher than projected. The radio and TV buzz I had hoped for never materialized. Hundreds of people came to the show, not thousands. In the end, I lost a bundle. Five figures. The headlining band felt so bad for me that they canceled some of their hotel rooms just to save me a little cash. It was personally embarrassing and financially devastating. I did my best to keep that a secret at home too.

Initially, it seemed like my sure-fire, lucrative business proposition simply required a lot of money upfront in order to succeed. As it turned out, the only "fire" in the process was my incessant heartburn. And if anyone were getting rich, it certainly wasn't me. They say "it takes money to make money," and that's often true, but it's not a guarantee. Sometimes spending a ton of money is just a quicker way to go broke.

KNOWING VS. DOING

It is critical to know your market size and your potential customers. It's Startup 101. Literally every potential investor will ask you that question. They want to know that your idea has a large-enough market to scale and eventually earn them a significant return on their investment. It's easy to hypothesize that your total addressable market (TAM) is worth a billion dollars. Or ten billion. But theory is always simpler than proof. Actually reaching your target customers with your product or service is far more difficult and, of course, far more expensive.

Unfortunately, reaching those people is just the beginning. Reaching them without ever converting them is just throwing gobs of money in the trash can. The key is to somehow convince your target to try, and eventually switch to, your product. Extrapolating on the Zig Ziglar quote from the beginning of this chapter, there are five things—beyond awareness—that you will likely need to account for in order to get a sale.

Need. If a potential customer feels like they "need" whatever it is that you're selling, you're in a good spot. Whether or not the need is real is irrelevant, as long as your customer feels like it is. There are many reasons someone might feel like they need your product or service, including, but not limited to, safety, survival, convenience, and comfort.

Price. For some, all they need to make the switch from one product or service to another is a better price. Phone and cable/satellite plans frequently fall into this category. Most offer the exact same (or very similar) services, and price is the only differentiating factor. It is theoretically possible to charge more simply by marketing your service as "better" than the competition, but with no other distinct differences between you and your competitors, you might have to win by being the least expensive.

Urgency. There are individuals who only choose to act (or buy) when they feel like they have to. Creating urgency in your offering can encourage those who might otherwise be content waiting to go ahead and purchase now. Ironically, urgency is often created using one of the first two items on this list: need or price. Scarcity of your product and limitations on time can help create urgency that might not otherwise exist.

Desire. People will pay for things they truly want, and—if the desire is strong enough—they will often throw all other reasoning out the window. Apple products are a perfect example. They're expensive and simple, and there are many other gadgets that can do the same things for far less. Thankfully for Apple, none of that matters because people want their products, specifically, and are willing to stand in line (and pay through the nose) for them.

Trust. This one takes time and will likely *not* be what most startups hang their initial sales messages on. Eventually, sure. But immediately, no. It's also the hardest obstacle to compete with. If your potential customers highly trust your competition, it's going to take herculean efforts to convince them to switch. People will even pay more for inferior products if they implicitly trust the company selling them.

Whatever you want to call this process—sales, marketing, distribution, customer acquisition—it starts with knowing who you want to reach. But as we've discussed, knowing your target isn't even close to half the battle. In fact, it's not part of the battle at all. Having a target is simply deciding who it is you're going to fight. The real battle doesn't begin until you start shooting at it.

LESS IS MORE

Earlier, I mentioned an adage that my radio consultants used to share when it came to being on the air: "Take as much time as necessary, but as little time as possible." Ideally, you should be able to say what you want to say in an understandable, compelling, and relatable way without rattling on and on unnecessarily. Yes, it takes time to set the stage, provide context, and tell a story, but it's incredibly easy to ramble and wander and go off on pointless tangents in the process.

The same can be said for your company's spending: "Use as much money as necessary, but as little money as possible." Ideally, you should be able to accomplish what you want to in an efficient, effective, and productive way without significant, wasteful overspending. Yes, it takes money to get things done, but it's surprisingly easy to spend based on the budget you have rather than on the goals you're actually hoping to accomplish.

Some have branded this the "lean startup" model. Others just call it economical or thrifty. I call it necessary and smart. Regardless of whether you have millions in investments or are bootstrapping from your own bank account, operating as if you have little now is a wise strategy for ensuring you have much in the months and years to come.

While it sounds simple, frugality is an extremely difficult concept to implement, even in our everyday lives. You don't try to conserve fuel when you have a full tank of gas. You drink more than a twelve-ounce can when you're pouring from a two-liter bottle. You use a few extra squares of toilet paper when there's a new roll on the holder. Basically, when you have more, you use more. When you have less, you conserve.

The key here is to trick yourself into constantly operating under the guise of having less. For many startups, this isn't a problem. Funds are limited, budgets are tight, customers are few, and conservation isn't really an option as much as it is a requirement. However, many entrepreneurs' eyes have bugged out of their heads when they receive their first six-figure investment check, launching them into months of frivolous and unnecessary spending.

While it's not possible in all cases, there are many ways to conserve the precious dollars that you have. And in the start-up world, every dollar is precious, no matter how many are in your account. Look for interns instead of paid employees. Try grassroots marketing instead of traditional. Offer equity instead of (or in lieu of some) salary. Rent instead of buy. Use systems others have created rather than creating them on your own. Prove things in small, economical ways before attempting to scale them.

In a budget crisis at home, every expenditure is on the table—cutting cable, going out to eat less often, eliminating a vacation, even selling a car or downsizing the house. While it may seem unnecessary or excessive, there is wisdom in operating your startup in the same way. Act as if it is perpetually in a budget crisis. Every expenditure should be on the table. Meals and marketing, personnel and perks, conferences and conveniences. Every single line item. Every single day.

When money got tight at RINGR, we began looking at our expenses in terms of how many customers it would take to recoup them, rather than in actual dollars. It was an incredibly helpful and eye-opening exercise. For example, if an industry conference was going to cost $5,000 to attend (booth space, travel, food, marketing materials, etc.), we chose to look at it as 250 monthly customers (at $20) or 25 annual customers (at $200). The question was always, "Will this expenditure realistically bring in enough new business to justify the outlay of cash?"

Sometimes the answer was yes. Sometimes the answer was no. But the mission was always the same: spend what is necessary and not a penny more.

A REPEATABLE CYCLE

The early stages of getting your product to market are a maddening, confusing journey of trial and error. Emphasis on error. The ultimate goal for any company is to find a marketing and sales process that works well with a small budget, and then repeat that process over and over again with a larger amount of money. There's no point in allocating a majority of your marketing dollars to a method that hasn't been tested thoroughly and proven to be effective. And not just in general, but for your company specifically. There are plenty of "proven sales methods" out there, but what works for one startup won't necessarily show positive results for another.

If targeted Facebook ads provide noticeable traction with a few hundred dollars, ramp up that budget. If you're not seeing appreciable results with Google AdWords after a few months, try something else. If a personal endorsement from a radio personality proves to bring in high-quality, long-term customers for you, then find twenty more. Or fifty more. It's not rocket science.

The repeatable cycle you land on will depend on your company, your target audience, and the product being offered. Radio spots and TV ads work for some, but cast a very wide, nontargeted net. Blogs and conferences put you in front of very specific groups, but often very small ones. You can also try free (though potentially less effective) options like posting Craigslist ads, being actively involved in specific Facebook groups, launching an affiliate program, and encouraging word of mouth among your existing users. At RINGR, we once slapped branded stickers on boxes of Tic Tacs at a technology conference instead of investing in slick brochures or fancy thumb drives. They were affordable, unique, and led to discussions with numerous potential clients.

Ultimately, the importance isn't what the cycle involves, it's that (1) you have one and (2) it's effective. The good news is that, whether it's with a small amount of money or with stacks and stacks of cash, the cycle is always the same: find them, reach them, convert them, keep them. Repeat.

What could possibly go wrong?

IX

ROTATION

Try Not to Get Dizzy

A pivot is a change in strategy without a change in vision.
—Eric Ries

The pivot. It used to be called the fuck-up.
—Marc Andreessen

SINCE I WAS A KID, I HAVE BEEN FASCINATED WITH SPACE. From putting a man on the moon, to weightlessness, to how the planets orbit the sun, I've always found the entire science to be intriguing. If I weren't so tall, I seriously would have considered becoming an astronaut—though I think average grades, subpar motivation, and a dislike of Tang likely hurt my chances too.

My first real memories of NASA came when I was in second grade, as I sat in my classroom and watched the space shuttle *Challenger* explode in real-time. Since one of the astronauts was Christa McAuliffe—the first teacher to ever go to space—it seemed as if every school in America was watching. The tragedy of that day didn't lessen my interest, however. In fact, I feel like it inspired me to pay even more attention.

Over the years, I built a model of the solar system for science class. Thankfully, this turned out significantly better than the motor from Chapter 3. My parents also took our family to the space centers in both Houston, Texas, and Cape Canaveral, Florida. In Houston I was just four and nearly got lost wandering off to try on space helmets. They literally had to page my parents over the intercom to come get me. As an adult, I even spent some time at space camp in Huntsville, Alabama (miraculously without throwing up even once). It was amazing.

One of my favorite bits of NASA trivia I've learned over the years is this: For the Apollo 11 spacecraft, a one-degree change in course at launch would have meant missing the moon by more than 4,100 miles. The distance being traveled and the speed at which they were traveling meant a tiny error in the beginning would have led to a gigantic problem later.

It's easy to see this principle play out in our everyday lives too. Recently, I was driving and found myself reading a billboard on the side of the road. Ironically, it was an overly wordy "don't text and drive" sign, warning of the dangers associated with taking your eyes off the road. Of course taking your eyes off the road was a requirement to read their message.

Anyway, it was only a few seconds before I heard my tires go over the rumble strip on the shoulder. Unbeknownst to me, I had begun traveling the direction I was looking. When you're moving at seventy miles per hour, it only takes a small shift in direction and a few short seconds to nearly put you in the ditch.

THE GOOD, THE BAD, AND THE UGLY

Adjusting the direction or course of your company midstream is called a pivot. These pivots can be literally anything, including business-model changes, additional product offerings, adjusted (or completely new) target markets, and even entirely new products or services altogether.

Pivots are often necessary—and most every successful business has been through several of them—but pivots can also be dangerous. There is an inherent risk in venturing too far away from your initial business plan, and there is an even greater risk in pivoting so randomly or so often that you end up spiraling out of control.

As you consider the current and future direction of your startup—and whether or not to pivot—it's important to know the following:

1. Small shifts in direction or focus have an enormous impact on your company over time.

This principle has both hope and caution built into it. The hope comes in knowing that if things are bad, slow, or off-track at the moment, making the right adjustment(s) now can pay major dividends later. If you don't believe me, consider the following:

- Before deciding on video games and consoles, Nintendo originally produced everything from instant rice to vacuum cleaners to playing cards.

- Starbucks used to only sell espresso makers and beans, not fresh-brewed coffee or Frappuccinos.

- Twitter (previously Odeo) was originally a way for people to find and listen to podcasts. Realizing iTunes was taking over the market, Odeo employees were given two weeks to come up with a new direction.

- YouTube has always been a video service, but started as a dating platform where users could upload short videos about themselves.

- Honda used to make only motorcycles.

- Flickr was once an online role-playing game.

- Play-Doh was designed to remove black soot from the walls near coal heaters in the 1930s.

- Mr. Wrigley used to give away chewing gum with every sale of soap and baking powder until the gum became more popular than anything he was actually selling.

- Facebook was once FaceMash, putting two people's pictures next to one another on the screen and asking students at Harvard to vote on which one was hotter.

The caution, of course, lies in knowing that the wrong pivot (or too many too quickly) can just as easily send you and your company in the opposite direction, miles from where you want or need to be—just like the Apollo 11 spacecraft.

While it's fun to read the success stories of those who made the right turn at the right time, there are undoubtedly an exponentially larger number of examples that tell the opposite tale. Rather than acting as a catapult, the wrong move at the wrong time can act like one of those huge augers used for boring giant holes in the ground, spinning an organization so furiously into a downward spiral that there's no way to back out.

2. You tend to travel in the direction of your focus.

Like the first, this principle is also a double-edged sword. If you're focusing on the right things, your company will likely be headed in the right direction. If you're focusing on the wrong ones, it won't be long before you're veering off the road on a collision course with a telephone pole.

Many a leader has—easily and innocently—steered his or her company down the wrong path by focusing on tasks that appeared to be important but ultimately were not. In the 1960s, Charles E. Hummel wrote a booklet with the title *Tyranny of the Urgent*. While I could spend several pages summing up his premise, author and speaker Michael Hyatt does it incredibly well in just a few words: "If you don't have a plan for your time, someone else does."

Without a purposeful and deliberate strategy for what you are going to focus on and work toward each day, you will easily get sidetracked by things that other people tell you are urgent, but aren't actually important to your success. It is these distractions that will start inching (or catapulting) your company off course. Sometimes it's little stuff like bothersome emails or phone calls. Sometimes it's bigger-picture issues like developing a new product or revamping your marketing strategy. None of these things are inherently bad, but if they aren't the *right* things to be focusing on at the moment, each of these "urgent" tasks can have a negative impact on your company's direction.

An additional danger here is that startup life is rarely slow paced. From the moment a company is founded, hundreds of important decisions have to be made extremely quickly, which means being slightly off course can get you in trouble faster, leaving you with less time to correct your path. Pastor Andy Stanley says it well: "The faster you're moving the further ahead you have to look."

The point is, the right focus and prudent pivots will be the difference between success and failure. The wrong focus and ill-advised pivots (or too many too quickly) will just make you dizzy. And broke.

PHONE A FRIEND

I used to love watching Regis Philbin and *Who Wants to Be a Millionaire?*. If you don't remember, contestants on the show had to answer a series of increasingly difficult trivia questions for the chance to win a million dollars. With each question, the dollar amount they won increased. But their risk increased as well. If a question was answered incorrectly, all (or most of) the money won up to that point was lost. So, you either stopped where you were, took the money, and walked away, or you risked it for the chance at more.

Regis offered each person on the show three "lifelines" to use at any point when he or she got stuck. They could either ask the audience, phone a friend, or eliminate two of the four multiple-choice answers and go fifty-fifty. It was always fascinating to see how much trust a contestant was willing to put in the hands of a friend or fate or several hundred complete strangers.

While starting RINGR, I can't tell you how many times I was faced with a similar dilemma. When decisions had to be made that didn't have a clear answer—about web design, company strategy, product features, or whatever—I had a choice: Do I go with my gut and just choose a direction, or do I call up an advisor or send a survey to our potential customers to see what they have to say?

There's nothing inherently wrong with any of these strategies. Each can potentially be helpful and provide insight and wisdom for a founder. The trick is determining what to believe, who to trust, and which course of action to take once you have the data and opinions in hand. But like those contestants on *Who Wants to Be a Millionaire?*, you have a decision to make: How much faith do I put in the hands of others when the risk is entirely my own?

THE MODEL T

When I first set up my workspace at the OCEAN accelerator, I taped a small square picture of a Model T inside my makeshift cubicle. In the middle of the paper was a quote from Henry Ford that said, "If I had asked people what they wanted, they would have said faster horses." It is, by far, my favorite quote of all time. So much so that I recently commissioned a painting by an artist friend of mine with that quote as the focus.

Ford's point was simple: people don't necessarily know what they want. The world's first car would never have been invented if left up to the whims of a consumer rather than a creator. The lens through which most people look at life is clouded by what they know. It takes a true visionary—an entrepreneur—to see options that aren't immediately obvious, and no amount of polling or number of surveys is going to lead to a solution that is innovative and industry altering.

Above all, Ford's quote is an encouragement for entrepreneurs to lead with their hearts, to go with their gut, and to do what others simply won't or can't. Entrepreneurs aren't meant to be vote counters. They're not supposed to be compilers of opinion. They're leaders, they're dreamers, and the roads they take are rarely evident to anyone else.

Sometimes those roads are dead ends and lead to nowhere. But sometimes—with the right focus and direction—those roads lead to amazing, never-before-seen places that change the course of a company, or an industry, or a generation.

X

ADAPTATION

Just Keep It Alive

The Dip is the long slog between starting and mastery. A long
slog that's actually a shortcut, because it gets you where you
want to go faster than any other path.

—Seth Godin, The Dip

MY TWO BOYS ARE ABOUT TWENTY MONTHS APART. This
means they are usually best friends and occasionally mortal
enemies. When they were little (like two and four years old),
they loved swimming. And when I say swimming, I mean
jumping in the water, splashing a lot, and then sinking immediately to the bottom.

Once, on an overnight trip to a nearby hotel, the three of
us were playing in the pool. Since it was a somewhat im-
promptu stay, we didn't have any swim stuff with us (life
jackets, floaties, etc.), but that didn't keep us away from the

water. So I came up with a plan. One boy would sit on the side of the pool while I played for a few minutes with the other. Then we'd switch. The plan worked perfectly until, suddenly, it didn't.

While pulling my oldest through the water, pretending he was some sort of high-speed motorboat, I noticed that my youngest wasn't on the ledge anymore. After a split-second scan of the pool deck, I realized there was only one place he could be—in the water. Specifically, under the water. I think every parent has at least one moment in life where you assume the worst has happened to one of your kids. This was my moment.

With my oldest under one arm, I dove toward the spot where his younger brother had been sitting just seconds earlier. Miraculously, my outstretched arm found a human—my human—and I was able to pull him above water and safely onto the ledge. He was coughing and scared, but he was fine. It couldn't have been more than a couple seconds, but I'm willing to bet they were the longest few seconds of both of our lives.

As a dad, I've often felt like the real goal of parenthood is basically to keep my kids alive until they're able to fend for themselves. Give them a good foundation, point them in the right direction, don't let them drown, and hope like hell they survive until college.

Welcome to startup life.

THRIVING BY SURVIVING

When founding your company, it's perfectly natural in the difficult and stressful times to think you're the only one who is struggling. Just like with parenting. When you're in the middle of the grind, there can be a sense of isolation, frustration, and even despair. And it's nearly impossible to think about long-term success because, at the moment, you're in pure survival mode.

Michael Ketterer is a singer and former contestant on *America's Got Talent*. He and his wife have adopted numerous children with special needs, trying to provide hope in the midst of extremely difficult circumstances. In one episode of the competition, Ketterer said of these precious kids, "When you're surviving you can't dream." Whoa, talk about a statement.

The same can be said in the midst of entrepreneurship. Entrepreneurs are natural-born dreamers, and anything that gets in the way of being a visionary feels crippling. Unfortunately, fighting for startup survival frequently means ignoring the dream for a while. The dream is still there, of course, but it simply can't be your primary focus.

Imagine you are literally drowning. While a beach chair, an umbrella, and a fruity drink may be the ideal end result for you, that's not what you're thinking about while thrashing around in the water. Trying to keep your lungs full of air and not full of water is slightly more critical. The margarita can wait.

When you're drowning as a founder, the same idea applies. A multimillion-dollar exit or IPO might be your ultimate dream, but that can't be what you're focused on, initially. At the moment you just have to survive until tomorrow, to make payroll on Friday, to sell more next month than you did this month. Wall Street will still be there when you come up for air.

The truth is, most founders who fully realize their dreams are simply the ones who found a way to keep their companies alive longer than their competition. These are the rare individuals who manage to keep the lights on today and then tomorrow and then the next day until, eventually, they find a bit of momentum. Unfortunately, like parenting, this almost always requires extreme sacrifice, an abundance of patience, and more than a handful of sleepless nights. Fortunately, the end result is more than worth it.

THE DIP

While an occasional company or two launches and sees immediate success, the vast majority are faced with surviving before thriving. There will likely be far more time spent hunting for the elusive "wabbit" like Elmer Fudd than playing in piles of money like Scrooge McDuck. It's a concept that author and business blogger Seth Godin calls "the dip." In fact, he wrote an entire book about it.

Essentially "the dip" is the discouraging, difficult, "we're probably not going to make it" period of time between launching your product and ultimately seeing it gain traction and market acceptance. In Godin's words, it's "the long stretch between beginner's luck and real accomplishment."

The beginning, before the dip, is fun. It's new and it's exciting, and it's where most founders love to live. It's where creation and dreams collide. It's whiteboards and bagels and ping-pong. Headphones and laptops and endless trips to Staples. In a relationship, you might call it the honeymoon period.

Unfortunately, as with marriage, the startup honeymoon ends too. Problems pop up. Disagreements happen. Progress takes more time and more energy than you thought. The vision of what could be morphs into the reality of what is. It's when you learn that starting is easy, but maintaining, persevering, and succeeding are hard.

When you find yourself in the dip (and you will), there is a decision that must be made: Do I continue or do I quit? The dip is single-handedly responsible for pretty much every quitting story ever. Lack of money, time, or acceptance? That's the dip. Waning motivation, investment, or support? That's the dip too. Distraction, confusion, or competition? It's the dip.

Quitting *is* an option. It's always an option. But should you? Godin puts it this way: "Quit the wrong stuff. Stick with the right stuff. Have the guts to do one or the other."

THE RESET BUTTON
Back in junior high and high school, my best friend, Rob, and I played video games. A lot of them. The Nintendo 64 was our console of choice back then, and we would sit in front of the television for hours on end racing and battling and hopping our way through a variety of different games. But we didn't just want to play these games. We wanted to win, we wanted to break records, and we wanted to do it

faster, better, and more dramatically than we had the time before.

Frequently, if we started a game that wasn't going our way or wasn't going to allow us to finish with the time or score we wanted, we'd hit the reset button. Scrape a wall on a hairpin turn? Reset. Get hit with a fireball saving the princess? Reset. Put the wrong block in the wrong opening? Reset. It was a quick and easy way to erase our mistakes instead of having to work hard to overcome those errors.

While it was just harmless fun for a couple of teenagers, I fear that this "reset" mentality may be tainting an entire generation of entrepreneurs. Technology has taught us that quitting is the fastest way to eliminate obstacles, ignore failure, and avoid adversity. Run low on funding? Reset. Get harsh criticism on your beta? Reset. Launch a failed product? Reset. It's quick and easy, and—unfortunately—common.

Resistance, mistakes, and failure are hardly reasons to quit something. In fact, they're actually reasons *not* to quit. Resistance builds strength—ask any bodybuilder. Hard work makes victory sweeter—ask any athlete. Success without setback is nothing but a myth, perpetuated by a video-game generation who were raised by helicopter parents, who try to eliminate challenges at every turn and believe everyone deserves a medal. But real success stories are almost never found by resetting, but rather by regrouping, reworking, and rethinking when challenges arise.

AVOIDING THE CROWDS

If you've ever gotten your vehicle stuck in the mud or the snow, you understand the principle behind the dip. When the wheels of your car begin to sink into what was once flat, solid ground, it can be a helpless feeling. To successfully move forward again, there are a number of techniques that *could* work, but there is no guarantee of what *will* work.

Sometimes momentum can carry you through the rut. Sometimes pressing the accelerator will pop you up and out of it. Sometimes stopping and adding sand will help you gain better traction. Sometimes having a friend stand behind the car and push will do the trick. And sometimes these things just make the ground softer, the rut deeper, and the vehicle even more stuck than it was before. It is all too easy for the dip to become a hole.

As it pertains to your company (rather than your car), you can cut your losses and quit, or use every trick in the book to get yourself to the other side. You can abandon your dream and start over with a new one, or find a way out of the dip with the dream you have now. The dip is littered with abandoned ideas and dreams because few ever get through it. It is far easier to leave than to fight. It's simpler to start over with a clean slate than to overcome challenges and mistakes. And sometimes that is the best option. But sometimes it isn't.

While persevering is difficult and messy, it puts you in extremely rare company and leaves you light years ahead of your competition. Yes, you can press the reset button, but as with video games, it takes you all the way back to the beginning. To the opening credits, to a fresh set of lives, and to the easy levels you can beat in your sleep.

But guess what else is back at the beginning? Everyone else.

XI

REFLECTION

The Man in the Mirror

Success is to live your life with integrity and not give in to peer pressure to be something you're not. Follow your passion, stay true to yourself, never follow someone else's path; unless you're in the woods and you're lost and you see a path, then by all means, you should follow that.

—Ellen DeGeneres

During the 2016 presidential campaign, no fewer than ten candidates alluded to—or outright said—that God had called them to run for office. Mike Huckabee, Michelle Bachmann, Rick Santorum, and numerous other politicians made these types of claims. The supporters of each loved the assertion. The detractors of each mocked it. It was politicking at its finest.

Regardless of political affiliation, many people suggested these candidates were out of their minds. It was obvious that they couldn't all be correct—they couldn't all have heard the exact same thing from God, could they? Since only one person could become president of the United States, it meant that most (if not all) of these politicians hadn't actually heard from God. Or if they had, their god was sorely mistaken, completely confused, or playing a cruel joke. And that doesn't sound like much of a god at all.

Were any of these politicians actually told by God to run for president? Honestly, I have no idea, and, at least for the sake of this discussion, it doesn't really matter. But there is a second question to ask, which is far more complex and far more profound: Is there a reason to run for president other than winning the election? And I believe the answer is, unquestionably, yes.

Setting aside your beliefs on God and/or the likelihood that our politicians hear from him on any sort of regular basis, it's important to recognize that—depending on your viewpoint—winning the presidency isn't the only successful outcome of a campaign, nor would it be the only reason God might ask someone to run.

For instance:

- Maybe the 2016 election was simply experience and exposure that laid the groundwork for a future victory.

- Maybe it was meant to be a learning experience for the candidates. One that helped them realize where their energy was truly needed, perhaps locally or regionally, instead of nationally.

- Maybe their unique perspective began a public conversation about an important topic that would never have been started otherwise.

- Maybe the spotlight led to a lucrative job as an executive somewhere outside of politics.

- Maybe the entirety of their run was simply to inspire and provide hope (albeit temporarily) for a small group of supporters in the midst of a trying, difficult time in our country's history.

My point is, winning the election wasn't the only way that the journey of these candidates could have a successful outcome, or a meaningful impact on themselves, their supporters, and society as a whole. While each politician's goal was likely the same, their individual definitions of success didn't have to be. In fact, it is possible—no doubt, likely—that these men and women each found meaning, fulfillment, and contentment in *not* winning. Perhaps even more than if they were sitting in the Oval Office.

WHAT IS YOUR WHY?

An entrepreneur's life is filled with thousands of decisions, but few are more important or more lasting than the decision on how to end. For startups that don't see much investment or traction, the answer to this question is quick, forced, and unpleasant. For those that see progress, it is a far more carefully considered, and hopefully enjoyable, process.

If your company's metrics continue to move up and to the right, you'll eventually be faced with a series of difficult decisions. Do I keep running and growing my company, or do I sell? If I sell, do I stay on the team or do I leave? Is there a way to keep creative control with new ownership? Do I even want that? When should (or can) we go public?

As with nearly every other part of your startup journey, there is no "right" answer for everyone. But there will be a right answer for you, your team, and your investors. The key is to find it. And, more importantly, to know *why* it's the right choice.

Most, if not all, entrepreneurs will admit that they dream of making millions from the sale of their startup or from executing a lucrative initial public offering (IPO). However, as you might imagine, a very small percentage of founders find themselves in such a position. According to *Forbes*, one out of ten startups succeeds. Success, however, simply means staying in business long enough to be profitable. By this definition, barely making payroll and rent with a few dollars left in the bank is technically "succeeding." However, if a multimillion-dollar exit is what you're after, the percentages are infinitely less favorable than one in ten. Emphasis on "infinitely."

Feeling successful at the end of your startup lifecycle will likely depend on your reasons for launching the company in the first place and your perspective on the road you've traveled since then. What was your *why?* Why did you risk everything to create your own enterprise? Was your goal to make gobs of money, to help people, or to revolutionize an industry? Were you trying to make a name for yourself, find work after being laid off, or to stretch the wings of your entrepreneurial spirit?

While the odds of making millions aren't quite as minuscule as becoming president of the United States, they are incredibly slim. The good news is, just like for political candidates, there are a variety of ways to find meaning, fulfillment, and success in your journey— regardless of the ultimate outcome.

ENJOY THE JOURNEY

I spent four years in my high school's marching band. While the stereotypical "band nerd" insults were frequently lobbed at me and my fellow musicians, we didn't care much. The primary reason? Our band was good. Really good. In fact, during my tenure I can't remember the Mahomet-Seymour Marching Bulldogs losing a single category in a single competition. We were the equivalent of four-time state champions, and culminated our amazing run with a trip to perform in the Rose Parade in Pasadena, California. No sports teams in our area even came close to that kind of success.

At the beginning of every school year our band director, Mr. Watkins, would draw a diagram on the chalkboard. It was an upward-sloping curve, getting increasingly steep as the line progressed. His motivational speech always went something like this:

*Band, we are about to embark on a journey together.
Early on we will see a lot of progress quickly. We will
memorize our music and our formations and, in a matter
of weeks, will transform from chaos on the field to
recognizable melodies and organized visuals. However,
as we move on, it will be more and more difficult to make
noticeable improvements. The little things, like dynamics,
precision, and intonation, make a huge difference—but
they are hard to master. Making something good is easy.
Making something great is difficult. But in the end,
whether we win or lose, as long as we progress, learn
from, and enjoy our journey, this year will be a success.*

Mr. Watkins's speech was always predictable and rehearsed,
but it was entirely true. And looking back, it didn't just
apply to music and marching. It can be applied to almost
anything. Well, anything worth doing, anyway. Mountain
climbing, painting, gardening, parenting, golf . . . and, of
course, launching a startup.

HEART MOTIVES

Years ago, a friend of mine walked me through something
called "heart motives." It is essentially the theory that people can act or respond to the exact same situation in the
exact same way, but for entirely different reasons. And it all
depends on whether, deep down, a person wants other people to love them, like them, respect them, or think they're
perfect. It is a helpful, yet perhaps overly simplistic, way to
understand what holds value to you as a person and why
you put such weight on it.

Let's say you hit the game-winning shot in a high school basketball game. Years later, what you remember the best and cherish the most is based entirely on your heart motive. To better explain, here are four hypothetical descriptions of the moments following that shot as told by people with the four different heart motives.

1. **Love.** "When I saw the ball go through the net and heard the buzzer go off, everything was a blur. I just remember standing there, arms raised, looking at my parents in the stands. Mom had tears in her eyes, my sister was jumping up and down screaming, and as I walked out of the locker room, Dad gave me a huge hug."

2. **Like.** "When I saw the ball go through the net and heard the buzzer go off, everything was a blur. I just remember my teammates mobbing me and carrying me off the court on their shoulders. The crowd was still going crazy and chanting my name. The next day at school was insane. It was all anyone could talk about. I even got my picture in the school paper that week."

3. **Respect.** "When I saw the ball go through the net and heard the buzzer go off, everything was a blur. I just remember the looks on the faces of the other team's players as they walked off the court. They were stunned, angry, and completely dejected. They thought they had us beat and

had been talking trash the whole game. It was so amazing to put them in their place."

4. **Perfect.** "When I saw the ball go through the net and heard the buzzer go off, everything was a blur. I just remember coach saying that the play was going to work, and we ran it exactly like he drew it up. I made my defender think I was cutting to the basket and then, at the last second, I stepped back, got the ball, and stroked a beautiful jumper—just like we had been practicing."

Your journey is unlike anyone else's. Your personal motivations are unique to you. And, ultimately, whether or not you find value in your journey is entirely up to you. Whether or not you see your endeavor as successful depends on your perspective. We all have different lenses, different mindsets, and different ways to find meaning and fulfillment in life. Your outcome doesn't have to be the same. Your bank account doesn't have to be equal. Your story doesn't have to look like everyone else's.

At RINGR, our journey isn't complete yet. At least not as of the writing of this book. We're steadily, but slowly, growing. We have a small but capable staff. We have lofty but attainable goals. And we have no idea what the future ultimately holds. But, personally, my joy has been found in the journey. Sure, I'd rather be acquired than go bankrupt, but the process has been worthwhile regardless. The worry, the work, the U-Haul—even the countless five-hundred-mile round-trips to see my kids during the divorce. I wouldn't trade them. Even if we had to shut the company down tomorrow.

IT'S THE MIDDLE, NOT THE END

Because the future hasn't happened yet, it can be easy to let every part of life feel like the end of your story. Failure and fear, debt and downsizing, rejection and retooling, pivots and pain—all of it, in the moment, feels like the end. But it's not, it's only the middle.

There is a difference between the end of a chapter and the end of a story, and your story isn't over yet. Even if you're having to close up shop, sell your company for pennies on the dollar, or look for a nine-to-five job, you're only in the middle of your story. While it can be difficult to realize that the end of this chapter may be near, it's critical to remember that there is far more to be written in your book. The journey is in the process, which has most assuredly been a breathtaking, lesson-filled, life-changing experience.

Until you're dead, everything is the middle.

XII

CONCLUSION

So What?

*The only thing worse than starting something and failing . . .
is not starting something.*

—Seth Godin

EACH SUNDAY, NEAR THE END OF HIS MORNING MESSAGE, A PASTOR FRIEND OF MINE USED TO ASK HIS CONGREGATION, "SO WHAT?" After twenty to thirty minutes of digging into a two-thousand-year-old book filled with somewhat outdated language and confusing metaphors, Tom wanted his audience to take a few minutes to process what they had heard. More importantly, he wanted them to determine how that information could impact their daily lives.

And so, in the waning minutes of his time on stage, Tom would recap his message, doing his best to directly apply those principles and directives to the here and now. He was keenly aware that if his congregants didn't have an obvious and immediate application for his words, he might as well not have said them at all. Their time (and his) would have been far better spent watching football, working in the garden, or going out for Sunday brunch.

Knowledge without action is entirely useless.

Learning for the sake of learning might be a fun hobby, but it is rarely a recipe for changing the world. Reading a book, underlining stuff, and bookmarking pages is great, but if none of it inspires movement, progress, or change, then it's just a colossal waste of time and paper.

And so, after all of the stories, tips, and lessons you've read in these pages, I ask the same question as my friend Tom: So what? What are you going to do or change or believe that is noticeably different than before you started? What can you do right now, this week, this month, that will positively impact your entrepreneurial journey?

EMBRACING INADEQUACY

Hopefully, after reading this book, you know more now than you did before. Hopefully, you feel more equipped to jump into—or continue—startup life. Hopefully, you have discovered powerful takeaways and helpful insights, and are already thinking through how to implement them. However, if I had to leave you with one lasting piece of advice, it would be this: be both willing and prepared to fully embrace your own inadequacy.

By *embrace* I don't mean ignore or avoid, but rather expect and accept. It's not natural for anyone to charge straight ahead when they think they're the dumbest person in the room. Normal people go find something else to do, something that's more comfortable or seems easier. Sane individuals tend to avoid fear, insecurity, and pain. But as we've established, entrepreneurs are far from normal or sane. We take pride in going against the grain, in facing adversity. We revel in doing things like they've never been done before, with the hope of one day creating something of significance.

It is possible to be the dumbest person in the room and yet the wisest person in the room, all at the same time. While many entrepreneurs may lack the business knowledge and background that launching a startup requires, they can more than make up for it with desire and determination and direct experience in the area they're trying to revolutionize. And the best part? Each of these attributes is incredibly attractive to investors, strategic partners, and, ultimately, customers.

If everyone who felt dumb or "less than" simply decided not to pursue whatever made them feel inadequate, nothing would ever change. Many companies wouldn't exist. Many people wouldn't have the rights they do today. Certain countries would never have tasted freedom. But, thankfully, history shows us the countless brave individuals—who likely felt as dumb and unprepared and unqualified as you sometimes feel—who decided to take a chance and embrace their inadequacy, despite the inherent risks.

SO WHAT?

Ideally, you are now inspired, informed, and more than a little excited to get started (or keep going). But there can be a fine line between being ready to jump into startup life and being ready to jump off a cliff. This emotional battle is terrifying, yet normal. Unsettling, yet routine. And so, before you embark on this journey of a lifetime, it's critical that you be unwavering in your answers to the following questions:

- Are you willing to risk your comfort now for the possibility of a realized dream later?

- Are you able to walk away from the familiar and into the land of the unknown?

- Are you okay with working harder than ever before with no guarantees of a payoff?

- Are you up for riding the startup roller coaster for the sake of your dream?

- Are you cool with feeling like the dumbest guy (or girl) in the room—maybe *every* room—for a while?

- Are you confident that the "uncomfortableness" will be worth it in the end?

And, perhaps most importantly . . .

- Are you going to regret it forever if the answer to any of these questions is no?

If you are anything like me, then these answers are simple, though not easy. Common sense may say one thing, but your entrepreneurial spirit says another. Friends and family may want safety, but something deep down inside you demands risk. Society may be content with complacency, but the very idea makes your skin crawl. This is the plight of every creator.

Who cares if you don't know enough code or make enough money or have enough schooling? Who cares if everyone else seems smarter or more qualified or better equipped? Who cares if the odds or the percentages or the math aren't in your favor? There can be no more excuses.

Take a risk. Change the world. Dumb doesn't matter.

About the Author

After spending nearly twenty years in radio, Tim J. Sinclair accidentally started a startup and is now the CEO of RINGR, a tech-based company that helps pre-recorded broadcasts and podcasts sound better. Tim's ultimate goal, however, is creative and effective communication. So, in addition to his continued work in radio, writing, and CEO-ing, Tim is the co-host of a one-hour lifestyle television show in Illinois, the host of the podcast "Also Humans," and the public-address voice of the Indiana Pacers, the Chicago Fire, and the University of Illinois.

www.ingramcontent.com/pod-product-compliance
Lightning Source LLC
Chambersburg PA
CBHW071707210326
41597CB00017B/2381